WRITERS AND THEIR W

ISOBEL ARMSTRONG
General Editor

ANTONY AND CLEOPATRA

Cleopatra's death scene (Act 5, scene 2), from the 1972 RSC production, Stratford-upon-Avon.

William Shakespeare

ANTONY
AND
CLEOPATRA

Kenneth Parker

Second Edition

NORTHCOTE
●● BRITISH
●● COUNCIL

© Copyright 2000 and 2005 by Kenneth Parker
Second edition 2005

First published in 2000 by Northcote House Publishers Ltd, Horndon House,
Horndon, Tavistock, Devon PL19 9NQ United Kingdom.
Tel: +44 (0) 1822 810066 Fax: +44 (0) 1822 810034.

British Library Cataloguing-in-Publication Data
A catalogue record for this book is available from the British Library

ISBN 0-7463-1140-0

Typeset by PDQ Typesetting, Newcastle-under-Lyme
Printed and bound in Great Britain by
The Baskerville Press, Salisbury, Wiltshire, SP1 3UA

For Gabrielle, again

Contents

Illustrations

Acknowledgements

While they must, at once, be absolved from all blame, I am nevertheless mindful of the obligation I owe to colleagues whose friendship and advice have been especially valuable in particularly liminal moments in the making of what follows. First, when the collapse of the apartheid state in South Africa enabled me to accept an invitation to return to the land of my birth for the first time since leaving there in a bit of a hurry at the end of 1964, and to the University of Cape Town in order to teach a Shakespeare course to students vastly different in colour as well as ethnic background from what had been the norm when I had been a student there. For that invitation, and for their unstinting kindnesses, I am especially grateful to two friends of very long standing: J. M. Coetzee and Dorothy Driver. Second, the privilege of being invited by Alessandra Marzola to the Universita degli Studi di Bergamo where, together with herself, Catherine Belsey and Angela Locatelli, I participated in a number of quite delightful research seminars devoted to the play and also made contact with Italian scholars at the beginning of academic careers, notably Giuliana Iannàccaro and Alessandro Vescovi. It was those two invitations which enabled me to try out some of the propositions being advanced in this brief chronicle.

That the opportunity for some of the experience that led to the invitations might be traced to journeys that had their origins in visits that had been made under the aegis of the British Council is perhaps one of the more delightful – and, at first sight, paradoxical – outcomes of a politics of cultural encounter for which our play is a paradigm case whose concerns reverberate tellingly in the present: not only 'abroad', but also 'at home'. Unquestionably, my greatest thanks are to colleagues in the

United Kingdom: Catherine Belsey, John Drakakis, Terence Hawkes, Kathleen McLuskie and Susan Wiseman; and especially to Tom Healy and Jerry Brotton who read variant drafts with meticulous care as well as generous advice.

To do this kind of work requires the assistance of key professionals: in this case, chiefly the specialist staff of the British Library and wonderfully helpful archivists: Marian Pringle at the Shakespeare Birthplace Centre Library in Stratford-upon-Avon; Nicola Scadding at the National Theatre archives, Sue Evans at the English Shakespeare Company, and Sarah Morris at the University of Bristol Theatre Collection. Special thanks to Peter Hamilton, eminent jurist and cultural arbiter, whose friendship dates (appropriately) from first encounters in Egypt many years ago, for documentation from his private archive of handbills about Prospect Theatre Company productions at the Old Vic in London and at the Edinburgh International Festival in 1977.

Lastly (because it is foretold that the last shall be first) to Gabrielle who continues, with apparent equanimity, to humour (always with wise counsel based on a deep knowledge of things French) my continuing infatuation with (most now long dead) literary women and women in literature.

Note on the Text

All references to *Antony and Cleopatra* are to the World's Classics edition, *Anthony and Cleopatra*, edited by Michael Neill (Oxford and New York: Oxford University Press, 1994).

All other citations of Shakespeare texts are from *The Norton Shakespeare, based on the Oxford edition of The Complete Works*, general editor Stephen Greenblatt (New York and London: W. W. Norton and Company, 1997)

Editorial procedures

While I have followed Michael Neill's usage 'Anthony' in instances of direct quoting from the text of his edition, in all other instances I have followed what appears to have become current convention. Whether in single-text editions (Arden; Cambridge; Everyman) or collected editions (Norton; Yale), the tendency seems to be to spell the name without the 'h'.

Abbreviations

Adelman   Janet Adelman, *The Common Liar: An Essay on 'Antony and Cleopatra'*, (New Haven and London: Yale University Press, 1973).

Bullough   Geoffrey Bullough, *Narrative and Dramatic Sources of Shakespeare: The Roman Plays*, vol. 5 (London: Routledge & Kegan Paul, 1964).

Cantor   Paul A. Cantor, *Shakespeare's Rome: Republic and Empire* (Ithaca and London: Cornell University Press, 1976).

Fitz   Linda Fitz, 'Egyptian Queens and Male Reviewers: Sexist Attitudes in *Antony and Cleopatra* Criticism', *Shakespeare Quarterly*, 28:3 (1997), 297–316.

Hall   Kim F. Hall, *Things of Darkness: Economics of Race and Gender in Early Modern England* (Ithaca and London: Cornell University Press, 1995).

MacDonald   Joyce Green MacDonald, 'Sex, Race, and Empire in Shakespeare's *Antony and Cleopatra*', *Literature and History*, 5:1 (1996), 60–77.

Neill   Michael Neill (ed.) *Anthony and Cleopatra* World's Classics (Oxford: Oxford University Press, 1994).

1

Introduction: 'Behold and see'

Philo's opening exhortation to Demetrius, to 'Behold and see' (1. 1. 13) is uttered not only with an exasperated sense of regret that, in his opinion, an un-Romanlike excess had transformed his general 'Into a strumpet's fool'; it is also clearly intended as a signal to the audience about how it should respond to the events being enacted upon the stage. An immediate response by Demetrius is interrupted by the splendid spectacle of the entry of Antony and Cleopatra with attendants, and fanned by eunuchs. And when he does so a moment later, his answer reveals a reluctance to concede to Philo's assertion. The visual richness of the enacted spectacle thus immediately calls into question the confidence of Philo's words as the common perception of Antony held by his friends in the Roman ranks. Indeed, Philo's 'Nay, but...' suggests the existence of a longstanding but unresolved debate within those Roman ranks.

One effect of the contrast between visual spectacle and verbal assertion is that of forcing the audience into the recognition that, contrary to what is being asserted by Philo, there is no Roman consensus – not even within the ranks of those soldiers who see themselves as Antony's friends. If it is therefore partly in order to persuade the waverers such as Demetrius that Philo insists that his view of his general should prevail, it is also partly to talk himself into believing his own estimation. Even he is not absolutely sure. Against the Antony of memory whom he recalls, the one whose 'goodly eyes,/ That o'er the files and musters of the war/ Have glowed like plated Mars' (1. 1. 2–4), he evokes another: that not-Antony who 'comes too short of that great property'/ Which still should go with Anthony' (1. 1. 60–61).

1

Ranged against those two competing evocations of the past there are two others: that of the present – the Antony of the spectacle on the stage, the one who dismisses as 'beggary' the love that can be 'reckoned' (1. 1. 15), the one who refuses to see Caesar's messenger, and the Antony of the future, the potentially salvageable figure about whom Demetrius, while 'full sorry/ That he approves the common liar who/ Thus speaks of him at Rome' (1. 1. 61–3), still 'will hope/ Of better deeds tomorrow' (1. 1. 63–4).

The indirect but powerful invitation to the audience to identify with ways of seeing Antony as wished by one Roman, is undermined not only by the response of another Roman but even more so and particularly by events enacted on stage. The problems posed for interpretation by the combination of feats of *spectacular* artifice and self-conscious language is perhaps best shown in Cleopatra's vivid evocation of the consequences of being vanquished and thereafter submitted to the spectacle of being paraded in a Triumph in Rome:

> Saucy lictors
> Will catch at us like strumpets, and scald rhymers
> Ballad us out o'tune. The quick comedians
> Extemporally will stage us, and present
> Our Alexandrian revels – Anthony
> Shall be brought drunken forth, and I shall see
> Some squeaking Cleopatra boy my greatness
> I'th'posture of a whore.
>
> (5. 2. 214–21)

What the audience is therefore asked to 'behold and see' flies in the face of what it sees enacted on the stage, and is therefore not readily willing to concede. The Antony trading repartee with Cleopatra about how to value love is neither the plated Mars of memory whom Philo recollects nor the not-Antony who does not measure up to what he is expected to be. And not simply when he is in Rome, but especially when he is elsewhere, engaged in the process of extending that imperial state's expansionist reach. The actions of this Antony on the stage are not in conformity with the role expected of the colonizer. Furthermore, the queen, with her attendants, and with her eunuchs fanning her is clearly not the lustful gypsy of popular Roman perceptions invoked by Philo and so memorably blamed

2

as the cause of Antony's excesses in Plutarch's description of
her: 'the last and extremest mischief of all other (to wit, the love
of Cleopatra) lighted on him [Antony], who did waken and stir
up many vices yet hidden in him, and were never seen to any;
and, if any part of goodness or hope of rising were left him,
Cleopatra quenched it straight and made it worse than before'.[1]
Demetrius clearly still lives in hope (1. 1. 61–4). Comparing
action against word, word against word, action against action in
this very brief first scene therefore has the effect of driving the
contemporary audience back to question the very ways of seeing
the events enacted on the stage.

It is because *Antony and Cleopatra*, perhaps more than any
other Shakespeare play, challenges certainties about ways of
seeing in the very moment of their enactment that my objective
will be limited to a modest attempt at the uncovering of
influential different readings, in the specificity of their contexts
and thereafter to offer an alternative to those dominant (albeit
competing) readings. Since the extensive antecedent critical
history of the play precludes the possibility of offering either a
systematic or comprehensive account of ways in which the play
has been seen, my endeavour will be to concentrate upon ways
of seeing in the present, therefore of critical engagements with
the text as a test of the critical theories themselves. And what is
fascinating about such ways of seeing in the present is how
those readings are infused with a sense of imagined pasts – as
Catherine Belsey argues so elegantly in *The Subject of Tragedy*, a
study whose seemingly conventional title is immediately
undermined by the subtitle, *Identity and Difference in Renaissance
Drama*:

> History is always in practice a reading of the past. We make a
> narrative out of the available 'documents', the written texts... we
> interpret in order to produce a knowledge of a world which is no
> longer present. And yet it is always from the present that we produce
> this knowledge, from the present in the sense that it is only from
> what is still extant, still available, that we make it; and from the
> present in the sense that we make it out of an understanding formed
> by the present. We bring what we know now to bear on what
> remains from the past to produce an intelligent history.[2]

2

Theories:
'All length is torture'

INTRODUCTION

Shakespeare was not the only dramatist who presented Roman history on the English stage. Other plays during the period included, for instance: Thomas Lodge, *The Wounds of the Civil War* (1594) which relocated Christopher Marlowe's *Tamburlaine* (1587) in Rome in the time of the dictator Sulla (138 BCE–78 BCE), and Ben Jonson, in whose *Sejanus* (1605) the operation of political power under the rule of the second Roman emperor, Tiberius (42 BCE–CE 37) was evoked with such acuity that the dramatist was hauled before the Privy Council on a charge of treason. It is likely that when dramatists of the time located their plays either in the past, or spatially outside the England of Elizabeth I and James I, that was one way of finding a solution to the problem of presenting the social crises of their own time on the stage. But to do so was dangerous. Ben Jonson and George Chapman were sent to prison (albeit only briefly) because the authorities deemed the anti-Scots jokes in *Eastward Ho* to be 'politically incorrect'!

Bear in mind that the period was one of recurrent political unrest. To cite some obvious examples: the revolt of the Anglo-Irish landowner Gerald Fitzgerald, which became known as the Desmond Revolt (1579–83); the Throckmorton Plot (1583) whereby (it was alleged) Mary Queen of Scots was to be placed on the English throne, an accusation that culminated not only in the beheading of Throckmorton and the expulsion of the Spanish ambassador Mendoza, but also in the beheading of Mary herself (1587); the role of the Earl of Essex in the colonization of Ireland, as well as of his subsequent execution (1601); finally, the event commonly referred to as the 'Gunpowder Plot' (1605).

But if (as Octavius asserts in the play) rulers shared a sense of threat, they also clearly found appropriate means for manipulation of the record. What republican as well as imperial Rome and monarchical England had in common was the policy and process of the careful cultivation of an image of stability, notwithstanding such danger. T. J. B. Spencer[1] claims that it was likely that Shakespeare had begun to read, or might have reread North's 1579 translation of Plutarch (itself a translation from a French version), at the time that he had been writing *Henry V.* He cites, as evidence for his view, the famous comparison the Welsh captain Fluellen makes between Alexander of Macedon and Harry V, chiefly for the contrast he draws between Alexander 'being in his ales and cups' killing his friend Cleitus, while Harry 'being in his right wits and his good judgements, turned away the fat knight with the great-belly doublet' (*Henry V*, 4. 7. 35–42).

If the story of the 'fat knight', Falstaff, being turned away by a former friend, now the king, is an example of the dissemination of the story supportive of the myth of England's political stability, the contrast with Alexander of Macedon triggers the recollection of the part that monarch played in the history of Egypt. Not only was he memorialized in the name of the city of Alexandria, it continued, after his death, in the dynasty founded by the general Ptolemy, of whom Cleopatra was arguably the most famous member. What the *Henry V* reference also points to is the manner in which the English history plays display an interest in the codes of Roman martial conduct – not now for technical reasons having to do with warfare itself, but how those Roman codes could be formulated as political practices in Elizabethan and Jacobean England.

It is noteworthy that Spencer does not contextualize the moment of Fluellen's observation. What had given rise to the Welshman's horror had been the action of the French to 'Kill the poys and the luggage! 'Tis expressly against the law of arms. 'Tis as arrant a piece of knavery, mark you now, as can be offert, in your conscience now, is it not?' (*Henry V*, 4. 7. 1–4). That act, on the part of the French, in its turn, had resulted in the English king's order: 'Then every soldier kill his prisoners!/ Give the word through' (*Henry V*, 4. 6. 37–8). It was for that act of the English that Gower (yet another of the 'domestic foreigners'

5

who is a captain in the army of the English monarch) had praised the king: 'the King most worthily hath caused every soldier to cut his prisoner's throat. O, 'tis a gallant king!' (*Henry V*, 4. 7. 4–9).[2] The analogous situation in *Antony and Cleopatra* is where Octavius tells a messenger to 'Go charge Agrippa/ Plant those that have revolted in the van/ That Anthony may seem to spend his fury/ Upon himself' (4. 6. 8–10).

THE HUMANIST INHERITANCE

Notwithstanding such evidence, Spencer will instead insist that Shakespeare is 'not so much occupied with an imaginative historical reconstruction', but that 'he concentrates the dramatic attention upon the relation between the two characters, without losing his hold on the imperial background in which the two find their fate'.[3] 'Imperial background', according to this view, is then largely a set of different physical spaces in which more fundamental themes and issues as well as ways of arguing that have their foundations in Renaissance humanisms are addressed – and three in particular: those of 'love'; of 'Duty versus Desire'; of 'Rome versus Egypt'.

It is important to recognize the deep and tenacious roots of a critical tradition that privileges love of a very particular kind – for ever captured in the title of John Dryden's 1678 imitation of the Shakespeare predecessor: *All for Love, or The World Well Lost*. For the Romantics that love was transcendent in nature. For critics who argue the case in favour of the primacy of individual consciousness in the face of social convention, this play was paradigmatic. William Hazlitt, in 1817, has no doubts: the 'grandeur' of Cleopatra's death and the 'strength of her affections *almost* [my emphasis] redeem her faults'.[4] Coleridge, in the following year, uses almost identical words: 'the intensity of the passion is its legitimacy: such is the moral truth that emerges manifestly from the work...They love each other; and such is the grandeur of their love that we forget their crimes'.[5] The outcome is a peculiarly tortured logic: that, on the one hand, they (and Cleopatra) had done 'wrong'; on the other, in terms of unspecified theories of jurisprudence, those 'crimes' can be forgotten. Note: not forgiven! It is a view that, in the last

6

year of the nineteenth century, leads George Bernard Shaw to offer a comprehensive condemnation which is unsustainable by reference to the text:

> Shakespear's *Antony and Cleopatra* must needs be as intolerable to the true Puritan as it is vaguely distressing to the ordinary healthy citizen, because after giving a faithful picture of the soldier broken down by debauchery, and the typical wanton in whose arms such men perish, Shakespear finally strains all his huge command of rhetoric and stage pathos to give a theatrical sublimity to the wretched end of the business, and to persuade foolish spectators that the world was well lost by the twain.[6]

Shaw's is a critical view well lost: especially for the offensiveness of his delineation of Antony and (particularly of) Cleopatra. What followed, however, was a modernization of the theme of transcendent love – notably by means of a critical language that makes use of an excess of hyperbole allied to a descent into critical imprecision. The enormously influential mytho-Christian scholar, G. Wilson Knight, for instance, asserts that the 'spiritual quality of the love ... transcends the grossly sensual' and that 'our view is directed not to the grossly material alone . but rather to the universal elements of earth, water, fire, and music, and beyond these elements to the all-transcending visionary humanism which endows man [sic.] with a supernatural glory'.[7] But how does it help to be told that the play is 'not merely a story of a soldier's fall, but rather a spelled land of romance achieved and victorious; a paradisaical vision expressed in terms of humanity's quest of love'?

What needs to be remembered is not only that Antony and Cleopatra, as well as several others in the play, commit suicide, but that in Christian theology there is an absolute injunction against self-slaughter. To give Dryden his due, he had stated the matter quite unequivocally in the famous remark in his Preface to *All for Love* (1678): 'I doubt not but that the same motive has prevailed with all of us in this attempt; I mean the excellency of the moral. For the chief persons represented were famous patterns of unlawful love, and their end accordingly was unfortunate'. What is fascinating, therefore, is that only one critic since has stated the orthodox case. For Irving Ribner, 'Whatever triumph Antony and Cleopatra may achieve is in defiance of the Christian moral order, and that we should emotionally share in this sense of triumph while we perceive that it is rooted in sin is a reflection of the paradox which this play absolutely embodies'.[8]

Almost without exception, as far as I can tell, humanist critics, instead of asking of death where is thy stingalingaling, or grave thy victory, provide some quite remarkable reworkings of Christian doctrine. To take two influential examples of the tortured logic the critics had to deploy in order to circumvent engagement with the notion of sin and thereby to underpin their support of the notion of death as 'triumph' over mortality – S. L. Bethell and Henri Fluchère. Bethell quite correctly reminds the reader that, according to the Bible, 'the strong sinner may enter Heaven before the prudential legislator'. But what could he possibly mean – either in terms of the theology, or of critical commentary – when he goes on to say that 'In *Antony and Cleopatra* the strong sinners meet their purgatory here. They do not desire or seek it; it is forced upon them from without – grace which visits them in the guise of defeat. Changes of character inexplicable by psychological determinism are readily explained if we perceive that Shakespeare is applying theological categories. Earthly defeat is the providential instrument of eternal triumph'.[9]

According to Fluchère (praised by T. S. Eliot in his Foreword to the English translation)

> the empire breaks up, the armies and the navies flee, the general runs upon his sword, the queen seeks refuge in suicide. It is in appearance a great failure. Death once more seems the great victor. But it is only in appearance ... the earthly reverse no longer leads to the metaphysical impasse where in former plays the hero was destroyed. There is no longer a spiritual cataclysm. On the contrary, Antony's death is a triumph and Cleopatra's a transfiguration ... This does not mean that evil is finally laid low, or that the serpent will no longer dare to show his head, but it does mean that he is no longer assured of being always the victor.[10]

Fluchère's exegesis is not only mistaken; his conclusions are misleading. Nowhere in Christian doctrine is there a view of the serpent as 'always the victor'. The serpent in the creation story has a very specific task: that of tempting Eve, whose 'fall' is offered as evidence of human sinfulness. Her punishment is for disobedience of God's commandment that had been relayed to her via Adam. It is that initial act (so the story goes) that provides the conditions which lead to the ruination of individuals caught up in unbridled excess of 'measure' – for which the female is to blame. The clearest statement of that position is by Benedetto Croce (1866–1952), in a text whose very title, *Ariosto, Shakespeare and Corneille*, intentionally seeks to provide the key markers of European literary culture. In his characterization of the play as a 'tragedy of the passions overpowering the will', Croce makes a distinction between what he calls a 'good' and an 'evil' will. And while he does not say so openly, there can be scant doubt that these are, respectively, male and female. The Italian original, as well as the English translation, insists upon the gendered dimension. The 'will', instead of exercising control over the passions, 'making its footstool of them', instead allows itself to be dominated by them. And although the 'will' searches after 'the good', it remains uncertain, dissatisfied with the path chosen. And it is that dissatisfaction with the objective that renders it incapable of making judgements. What should be noted, furthermore, is the rich sexually suggestive tone:

> A typical form of this first condition of the will is voluptuousness, which overspreads a soul and makes itself mistress there, inebriating, sending to sleep, destroying and liquefying the will. When we think of that enchanting sweetness and perdition, the image of death arises at the same instant, because it truly is death, if not physical, yet always internal and moral death, death of the spirit, without which a man is already a corpse in the process of decomposition. The tragedy of *Antony and Cleopatra* is composed of the violent sense of pleasure, in the power to bind and to dominate, coupled with a shudder at its abject effects of dissolution and death.[11]

In order to understand Croce's view of the play as a 'tragedy of passions', it is perhaps useful to mention the stress he places upon the premise that works of art are the outcome of the mental productions of uniquely individual makers. It follows, therefore, that the task of the critic is restricted to that of the clarification for the reader/audience of that text. And the parameters of that act of elucidation are also restricted: 'There is no other way than to follow out the individualizing method to the very end: to treat works of art not in relation to social history but as being each one a world in itself, each one, of its hour, receiving the inflow of the whole of history, transfigured and elevated by the power of fancy into the work of art which is a

9

creation, not a reflection and a monument, not a document'.[12]

The deliberate rejection of the historical and the political in essays which were first published in Italy in 1951 is here remarkable not simply because of the refusal to concede their centrality in the making of the drama, but also because of the critic's own personal history. Croce was not only an unsilenceable foe of Mussolini's fascism; afterwards, as participant in the making of the post-war Italian constitution, he refused offers to be head of the new democratic state. The case of Fluchère is more complex. His book apparently emerged from lectures he had delivered to his students in the university of Aix-en-Provence during the years of the Nazi occupation of France. That his text elides all reference to the political may well offer silent testimony to the protocols of academic conduct during a moment of foreign domination.

Such refusal to take into account the political may, of course, also be traced back to the distinction made between 'Literature' and 'Philosophy' that, especially in post-war Anglo-American humanist theory is made touchstone for aesthetic 'taste'. Morris Weitz is quite certain that 'in the case of *Antony and Cleopatra* we have a great tragedy which contains a number of philosophical themes but no implied or elicitable philosophical thesis or universal claim'. It is, rather, 'primarily a magnificent love story, full of exciting episodes, fascinating characters, marvellous, luscious poetry, and a traditional tragic theme in the rise and fall of great ones'.[13] It is themes such as these which are seen to have 'universal validity', and which are repeatedly advanced by some of the most influential post-war British and North American critics: L. C. Knights,[14], Franklin M. Dickey[15] and J. Leeds Barroll.[16] For all of them, to some extent or other, the dominant theme with which the play engages is that of the subversion of reason by passion. It is, they claim, a theme that was not only highlighted by the ancients, but one which, they insist, was shared by Shakespeare, who came down on the side of 'Rome' against 'Egypt'.

Here they echo Hazlitt, who was clear about the nature, but not the consequences, of choice along the faultlines of that binary: 'The play...presents a fine picture of Roman pride and Eastern magnificence. And in the struggle between the two, the empire of the world seems suspended'.[17] And A. C. Bradley had no reservations about where he stood: 'In *Romeo and Juliet*, *Hamlet*, and *Othello*, though in a sense we accept the deaths of hero and heroine, we feel a keen sorrow. We look back, think how noble and beautiful they were, wish that fate had opposed to them a weaker enemy, dream possibly of the life they might have led. Here we can hardly do this. *With all our admiration and sympathy for the lovers we do not wish them to gain the world. It is better for the old world's sake, and not less for their own, that they should fail and die*' (my emphasis). For that critic 'A man who loved power as much as thousands of insignificant people love it, would have made a sterner struggle than Antony's against his enchantment' by a Cleopatra who 'destroys him', 'ruins a great man, but shows no sense of the tragedy of his ruin'.[18] And that lack of consideration for him on her part might well be explained by judgement of George Brandes: 'Just as Antony's ruin results from his connection with Cleopatra, so does the fall of the Roman republic result from the contact of the *simple hardihood of the West with the luxury of the East*' (my emphasis).[19]

John F. Danby introduces a welcome whiff of balance into the argument when he suggests that ambiguity exists in Egypt, as well as in Rome. And such ambiguity, he insists, 'is the logic of a peculiarly Shakespearean dialectic. Opposites are juxtaposed, mingled, married, then from the very union which seems to promise strength dissolution flows'.[20] John Drakakis is therefore quite right in including an extract from Danby's essay '*Antony and Cleopatra*: A Shakespearean adjustment' as the first contribution to his 1994 *Casebook* on the play – an inclusion for which he offers the following justification:

Against the transcendental humanism of earlier criticism, which celebrated the spiritual love of Antony and Cleopatra, Danby locates the 'meaning' of the play in a more skeptical and dialectical ethos; for him the tragedy resides in *disjunction*, not ultimate unity, and the figure who represents this process above all is Antony, caught between the conflicting but irresolvable demands of Rome and Egypt...Where other critics have been content to gloss over the play's discontinuities, Danby, remarkably, makes them the very centre of his own critical argument, an argument that engages the audience in the dramatic process of problematising the act of judgement itself.[21]

11

PROBLEMATIZINGS

The break with humanist critical practice was neither swift nor simple – nor, indeed, a clean one. Thus, for instance, Terence Eagleton, in 1967, could claim that Antony and Cleopatra 'live throughout at this point: they are undone, they have touched the lowest point of abasement and dissolution, and are therefore in a position of desperate strength, capable of joy', with the result that it 'is about this kind of paradox, as it affects a whole relationship, and the play itself is at this point where its two central characters move, the point of balance between utter desperation and utter triumph'.[22] Having in the interim become Terry, by 1986 Eagleton offers what appears to be a more orthodox Marxist explanation – until it is recognized that the ethics are still those of the humanist Marx and that the critical language is that inherited from Wilson Knight and Bradley:

> In *Antony and Cleopatra* the traditionalist social order flamboyantly burns itself out, rots itself with motion, snatching a final arrogant victory from its own demise. Creative abundance and clogging superfluity become well-nigh impossible to distinguish. Unfit for social order, Antony and Cleopatra illuminate the meagre pragmatism of calculating Rome in the fire of their self-immolation. What the play's stonily realist characters have to say of the ageing lecher Antony and his shrewish strumpet Cleopatra is at once to the point and gloriously irrelevant. The language of politics no longer meshes with the discourse of value, and the play simply dramatises their contradiction...without seeking to resolve it.[23]

Overwhelmingly much more interesting and rewarding as critical practice has been the contribution of the 'monstrous regiment of women' critics whose writings, as well as their increasing presence in the academy, have helped transform the reading of the play. If pride of place must go to the classic 1997 article by Linda Fitz,[24] 'then it is also appropriate to remember a predecessor, Rosa E. Grindon (1930).[25] Now hardly known, but in her day a key figure in Shakespeare productions in Manchester by Richard Flanagan (and, after him, Frank Benson), Rosa Grindon's stature may be judged by the fact that she was invited to deliver a lecture at the Manchester Shakespeare Tercentenary celebrations. For her 'the men critics, in their sympathy for Antony, have treated Cleopatra just as Antony's friends did, and for the same cause. They seem to forget that, when Antony returned to Egypt, the minute his guardian angel, Octavia, left him, interrupting Cleopatra's buildings of temples (so history says), he brought equal ruin to her'. Small wonder that the editor to the posthumously published lectures (Grindon died in 1923, aged 75) felt the need to caution, in his Foreword, that 'With some of her conclusions the [male?] reader will not agree. It is important, however, to bear in mind that, as appears on the title page, these lectures were written from a woman's point of view and, as such, they introduce a new element into the study of Shakespearean drama'.

Rosa Grindon's editor may well have made more or less the same kind of remark about the intervention made by Linda Fitz. For Fitz (who mentions Grindon) the central issue is quite clear: 'Both the reduction of the play's action to "the fall of a great general" and the definition of the play's major interest as "transcendental love" make impossible a reasonable assessment of the character of Cleopatra. There is a word for the kind of critical bias informing both approaches: it is "sexism"' (Fitz, 297).

Fitz marshalls a detailed and devastating case. She is particularly deft in demonstrating the variety of tactics used: 'in male critical commentary on the character of Cleopatra an intemperance of language, an intensity of revulsion uncommon even among Shakespeare critics'.[26] One of those tactics is to describe Cleopatra as 'Woman'. Indeed, she is seen as the 'archetypal woman. practicer of feminine wiles, mysterious, childlike, long on passion and short on intelligence – except for an animal cunning' (Fitz, 298). Fitz also goes on to point out that if the arguments deployed above do not convince then these critics have a fail-safe – that of a double standard of measurement: 'what is praise worthy in Antony is damnable in Cleopatra. The sexist assumption here is that for a woman love should be everything: her showing an interest in anything but her man is reprehensible. For a man, on the other hand, love should be secondary to public duty and self-interest. Almost every scene in which either character appears has been subjected to this double-standard interpretation' (Fitz, 304).

In support of her argument, she uses three examples, to each of which I shall return later on: (1) the Thidias scene (3. 12), which male critics have tended to perceive as an attempt on

Cleopatra's part to save her political (perhaps actual) skin by appearing to make a deal with Octavius at the expense of Antony after the battle of Actium; (2) while Antony is criticized for his neglect of (Roman) public affairs, those same critics tend not to take seriously Cleopatra's attempts to participate in public affairs. Once again the Actium episode is singled out; (3) in the discussion of Antony's and Cleopatra's respective motives for suicide, critics tend to place a high value on his action, while doubting hers. Daniel Stempel, Fitz notes, 'coming upon the lines, "He words me, girls, he words me, that I should not/ Be noble to myself" (5. 2. 191–2) is indescribably shocked that Cleopatra speaks whole lines without reference to Anthony: "No word of Antony here. Her deepest allegiance is to her own nature"' (Fitz, 305).

Fitz offers a detailed rebuttal: 'If, however, we look at the play, we see that Cleopatra adduces the following reasons for taking leave of the world: (a) she thinks life is not worth living without Antony; (b) she sees suicide as brave, great, noble, and Roman; (c) she wants to escape the humiliation that Caesar has planned for her, and desires to have the fun of making an ass of Caesar; (d) she sees suicide as an act of constancy which will put an end to her previous inconstant behaviour and to the world's inconstancy which has affected her life; and (e) she wants to be with Antony in a life beyond the grave' (Fitz 305–6).

Given the critical engagement with the play by critics of the fifties, sixties and seventies, it is noteworthy that there is either very little (or more often, no) consideration of the play – and especially of Cleopatra – in many of the critical texts of great distinction which have appeared in the eighties – and especially in those which have to do with feminist theory and with history.[27] For instance, Lisa Jardine's *Still Harping on Daughters: Women and Drama in the Age of Shakespeare* (1983) has three brief references to the play. Even more noteworthy, there is no mention in her *Reading Shakespeare Historically* (1996). While commentary on Coppélia Kahn's *Roman Shakespeare: Warriors. Wounds and Women* (1997) will be offered later on, it should not go unnoticed that while, in her sophisticated *Man's Estate: Masculine Identity in Shakespeare* (1981) there are splendid commentaries on *Venus and Adonis, Romeo and Juliet, The Taming of the Shrew, Macbeth* and the history plays, Cleopatra is mentioned only once. And there, though the queen is made to fit into the model that Kahn develops, she seems to be mentioned only in order to signal her radical alterity from the other female figures: 'It goes without saying that Shakespeare portrays all his women characters as sisters, daughters, wives, or mothers; Cleopatra is only superficially an anomaly, for her milieu of Egyptian fecundity binds her profoundly to the human family through sexuality and procreation'.[28] Notwithstanding the demur, the act of inclusion here becomes one of marginalization.

And how to explain the absence from two collections issued under the Verso imprint in 1995: *Shakespeare and Gender: A History*, edited by Deborah Baker and Ivo Kamps, and the companion volume, *Materialist Shakespeare: A History*, edited by Ivo Kamps. That absence of a consideration of the play is even more noteworthy in the collection *Post-Colonial Shakespeare*, edited by Ania Loomba and Martin Orkin (1998),[29] even when it is recognized that the volume is constituted out of selections from proceedings of a conference. Lastly, the question has to be asked of Peter Erickson's *Rewriting Shakespeare. Rewriting Ourselves* (1991),[30] the first part of which is devoted to 'Shakespeare's representations of women', particularly since in his earlier *Patriarchal Structures in Shakespeare's Drama*, Erickson had introduced the notion of 'feminists who happen to be male, – an oxy-moronic notion if ever there was one. No matter how well-intentioned, about the best to which a male writer can aspire is to be a non-sexist critic.

And yet what needs to be added to reappraisals of Cleopatra is one that not only male critics, but Fitz also misses out on: that it is not simply because she is female that Cleopatra is constructed as Other. Above all she is conceived of as being that because she is 'Oriental'. It is to that aspect, at the intersection of the gendered and the postcolonial, that I now turn briefly to signal it as a key element of the story that will be developed in a later chapter. It is not so much that it is a matter that has not been addressed, but rather that the pronouncements which follow are often based upon misconceptions – and those misconceptions themselves built upon misreadings of the written records of those encounters. Thus, for instance, the conventional view is as stated by Linda Bamber: 'In a sense, of

15

course, there is little difference between Cleopatra as Egypt and Cleopatra as the Other, for it is *as* [her emphasis] Egypt that Cleopatra represents the Other. But in this reading Egypt and Rome are no longer equal but opposite options for the hero. In this reading Egypt is the new world, the world that calls into question all the old certainties, the heath on which Antony faces the indifference of the universe and his own falling off from what he means to be'.[31]

Once again, Cleopatra is made to carry the blame for Antony's indecision. Even more seriously, it is quite mistaken to suggest the distinction between Old World and New World to which Bamber refers as something that operated in Rome with reference to Egypt in particular, or the Orient in general. Such views, as Edward Said has shown, date from the late eighteenth century, from which 'roughly defined starting point Orientalism can be discussed and analysed as the corporate institution for dealing with the Orient – dealing with it by making statements about it, authorizing views of it, describing it, by teaching it, settling it, ruling over it: in short, a Western style for dominating restructuring, and having authority over the Orient.'[32] The often-quoted remark made by Rana Kabbani that 'For Antony, the East arrived in Cleopatra's barge. This was the East, the Orient created for the West',[33] is simply wrong. The so-called 'East' did not 'arrive' in Cleopatra's barge. As was the case with other places, it did not require, was not dependent upon, 'discovery' by others; it had pre-existed that moment. More importantly, what is required is that a much sharper distinction be made not only between 'East' and 'Orient', but also within the components of the category referred to as the Orient: between Turks; Persians; Egyptians, as well as varieties of Christians, to which Early Modern European diplomats, merchants and men of learning went because the Orient was where learning and culture were that some in Europe felt the need to emulate – or, at least, study.[34] The tales they told, speedily translated into the main languages of Europe, were regularly reprinted during the next 200 years as part of the project of Orientalism – much in the same way as directors in the theatre have, specially since the 1970s, made use of the pronunciations of the literary critics in the making of their stage productions.

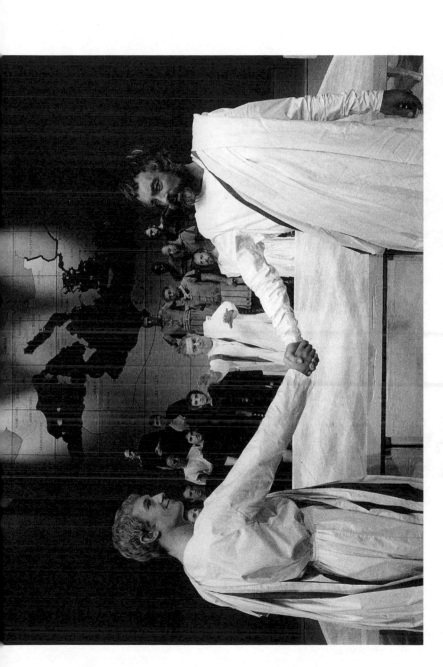

1. The Triumvirate: Octavius, Lepidus and Antony (Act 2, scene 2) from the 1972 RSC production, Stratford-upon-Avon.

2. 'Orientalist spectacle' (Act 1, scene 5), from the 1972 RSC production, Stratford-upon-Avon.

3

Rome:
'To drench the Capitol'

'SHAKESPEARE'S ROME'

M. W. MacCallum, in his monumental and imperious study of
the Roman plays (1910, reissued in 1967 with a Foreword by
T. J. B. Spencer), insists that while the dramatist had a sound
knowledge of his sources, and displayed great fidelity to those
sources, that

> does not mean that in the Roman any more than in the English plays
> he attempted an accurate reconstruction of the past. It may even be
> doubted whether such an attempt would have been intelligible to
> him or to any save one or two of his contemporaries. To the average
> Elizabethan (and in this respect Shakespeare was an average
> Elizabethan, with infinitely clearer vision certainly, but with the
> same outlook and horizon) the past differed from the present
> [meaning around 1910] chiefly by its distance and dimness; and
> distinctive contrasts in mariners and customs were but scantily
> recognised.[1]

Following MacCallum, subsequent studies fall into two
divergent, but often overlapping, groups. In the first, there is
the attempt to ascertain the extent of the dramatist's knowledge
of the classical world; in the second, particular attention is
devoted to language and imagery. The first group might be
represented by the following: J. E. Phillips (1940); J. A. K.
Thompson (1952); Reuben A. Brower (1971); J. L. Simmons
(1973); Paul A. Cantor (1976); Robert S. Miola (1983); Vivian
Thomas (1989) and Geoffrey Miles (1996).[2] Then, in the wake left
by the influential 1930 study by G. Wilson Knight, *The Imperial*

Theme,[3] the second category might include: Maurice Charney (1961); Ernest Schanzer (1963); Janet Adelman (1973) and John Wilders (1978).[4] The intellectual foundations upon which all these critics, to a larger or lesser extent, base their work can be traced back to Enlightenment ideas about 'progress', in which the work of two German scholars, August von Schlegel[5] and Hermann Ulrici,[6] is influential.

That notion of 'progress' was itself tied to a sense of particularly appropriate political structures. And those structures were, in their turn, seen as Europe's inheritance from Rome: which might account for (for instance) the observation and echo, almost exactly a century after Ulrici and Schlegel that

> the political action of the two plays [*Julius Caesar, Antony and Cleopatra*] ... is not only continuous in development, but consistent in philosophy and conformable to the principles of political thinking about the nature and structure of states generally accepted in Shakespeare's day... Out of the welter of divided and conflicting authorities emerges the one man who, according to the political standards of the Renaissance, is qualified to be the natural head of the Roman body politic. With nothing to indicate that the promise of civil peace and order will not be fulfilled, the political action of *Antony and Cleopatra*, unlike that of the earlier play, can end conclusively and happily, for the normal state-structure has been re-established.[7]

It is difficult to see on what basis it is possible to assert that the text demonstrates the inevitability of Octavius's eventual triumph. While what is portrayed on stage is broadly in line with the historical record, even more important it seems to me are the ways in which the dramatist hedges the events about with qualifications. The notion of 'natural head' of the empire is especially tendentious. Not only is there no textual justification for such a view, but such a reading simply ignores the matter of the means by which Octavius eventually achieved power. Finally, to speak of the play ending 'conclusively and happily' in the context of what happens on a stage that is eventually littered with dead bodies and against a background of battles in which many have died would seem to indicate a remarkably phlegmatic concern with detail. Above all, to speak of the 'normal' state-structure as having been 're-established' is a gross misreading of the text. In what I wish to suggest marks the moment of liminal encounter, the younger Pompey asks the question of his three adversaries about which not nearly sufficient attention has been paid.

> What was't
> That moved pale Cassius to conspire? And what
> Made all-honoured, honest, Roman Brutus,
> With the armed rest, courtiers of beauteous freedom,
> To drench the Capitol, but that they would
> Have one man but a man?

(2. 6. 14–19)

At least three features need to be noted about the question: (a) the language used to describe the conspirators. There must surely be an unmistakable irony in the comparison between the 'courtiers of beauteous freedom' and the second triumvirate facing the speaker. After all, Plutarch himself resorted to a similar literary device when he described Antony's victory at Philippi: 'the greatest and most famous exploit Antonius ever did in wars (to wit, the war in which he overthrew Cassius and Brutus) was begun to no other end but to deprive his countrymen of their liberty and freedom';[8]
(b) that the questioner goes on to explain why he had now gone to war against the Roman state. Since the issues that had forced his father into going to war against the first triumvirate, and being defeated by Julius Caesar at Pharsalus (48 BCE) had not been resolved, his intention now was 'To scourge th' ingratitude that despiteful Rome/ Cast on my noble father' (2. 6. 22–3);
(c) the quite remarkably dismissive response on the part of Octavius: 'Take your time'.

One attempted explanation was that given by J. L. Simmons (1973): 'Shakespeare accurately represents Rome as a pagan world in which the characters operate with no reference beyond the Earthly City. All attempts at idealistic vision by the tragic heroes, all attempts to rise above the restrictions of man and imperfect society, are tragically affected by the absence of revelation and the real hope of glory...Shakespeare views his Roman world with the cosmic irony of what that world could not know...The Roman heroes do not have access to St. Augustine's Heavenly City'.[9] Attractive as it seems at first sight, the argument is patently specious. The critique Shakespeare offers here of the operation of Roman power is not

19

located in the specifics of Christian theology – and certainly not as that theology was interpreted in Elizabethan and Jacobean England. Furthermore, Elizabethan and Jacobean audiences could cope with both pagan and Christian worlds – including those worlds on stage: for instance, that of a *Dr Faustus,* in which divine retribution is made manifest, as well as that of a *Tamburlaine,* where it is absent, despite the fact that the latter is one monarch who is obviously deserving of such divine retribution; yet he dies, unrepentant and apparently unpunished, lamenting desires of conquest unfulfilled.

Even if Gary B. Miles is correct in his assertion that 'The ancient world knew no such emphasis on interiority until St. Augustine, whose *Confessions* elaborated the implications of Christian belief that eternal salvation is contingent ultimately on the individual conscience',[10] that is not the issue in this play. Nor is the notion of 'order', much loved by so many critics. Geoffrey Miles, for instance, maintains that in *Antony and Cleopatra* 'that solidity has melted away', in evidence of which he claims that the 'paradigm case is the scene on Pompey's galley: the world rules drunk and dancing on a floating ship, unaware that at any moment the ship may be cut adrift and their throats casually slit'. But that is not so! Some of the world may be 'drunk to bed', but no throats are slit – at least not at that moment – and certainly not without those wishing to do so first seeking permission – which request is rejected (2. 7. 74–81). The really much more frightening moment of the delineation of political relations – frightening because disguised as evidence of amity – is of the encounter, a few scenes later, between Agrippa and Enobarbus. To the former's deliberately ironic framing of the question: 'What, are the brothers parted?', the latter responds with the news that *they* have *despatched* with Pompey and that the other three are *sealing*. But all that is temporary; the agreements being sealed will not last. And why? Because the real relationship between the three is that Octavius will win out: the others, as Enobarbus so memorably states it, 'are his shards, and he their beetle' (3. 2. 20), and as Cleopatra will echo: 'we/ Your scutcheons and your signs of conquest shall/ Hang in what place you please' (5. 2. 134–6).

While Geoffrey Miles is right to note that the word that dominates the politics of *Antony and Cleopatra* is 'fortune', and that

that word occurs no less than forty-six times in the play, he fails to point out that the real decisions are taken neither by nor in the name of an abstraction but by self-aggrandizing warlords in competition with each other. And even though Miles qualifies his argument with the observation that 'the distinctions between Rome and Egypt begin to blur and dissolve as Antony takes to Egyptian life, Pompey hopefully tries to put on an "Alexandrian feast" (2. 7. 94), and Dolabella is converted to the "religion" of Cleopatra's love (5. 2 198ff), while Cleopatra dies "after the high Roman fashion" (4. 16. 88)', his central case is still the old-fashioned one that 'The imagery enforces a contrast between Roman stability and Egypt's abandonment to flux: Egypt is associated with water, the tides, the overflowing fertility of the Nile; Rome with dry land and with symbols of restraint, control, and geometrical rigidity – the arch, the set-square, the unslipping knot'.[11] The binary, with Roman values implicitly preferred to those of Egypt, remain even when heavily qualified.

For Robert Miola: 'Initially, Rome appears to be a place of *gravitas* in conflict with Egyptian *voluptas*, but the dichotomy between these places and their values does not remain absolute and unqualified...Rome in *Antony and Cleopatra* is a kingdom [sic] divided against itself in bloody civil war. More important, however, the Empire is in spiritual conflict with itself, caught between its profession of honourable ideals and its sordid, self-serving practice.[12] Roman values are defined by Gary B. Miles as 'high public office, military victories, public benefactions – typically in that order'.[13] What he does not appear to see is that, in the play, such values, in practice, are marked by their breach. Comparison of their words with their acts will reveal that what constitutes the difference between Octavius, Antony, Lepidus and Pompey is the degree of success or failure of their deeds. Fortune may have a hand; but, ultimately, it is the power to be able to enforce the choices these warlords make that prove to be decisive. And the same situation applies, as well, to their assistants: Enobarbus; Ventidius; Dolabella. One explanation might well be that while their futures are explained by their differences, it is also determined by their imagination of the past. And in that past, there looms, for all of them, the figure of Julius Caesar: political precursor to all; sexual precursor to some. It is a point excellently made by Marjorie Garber who draws on

Freud's notion of 'the uncanny' and on other Freudian texts to seek to discover 'the ways in which repetition-compulsion, castration, transference, mourning all materialize and dematerialize the Shakespeare text'.[14]

Reference to Julius Caesar leads to an inevitable comparison: not now between Rome and Egypt, but between the Rome of the republic and that of the empire. Cantor makes the case well. In the republic, he asserts, participants 'display their devotion to their city repeatedly, whether they are talking to themselves or at the public forum, in moments of heated passion or studied reflection'. Making use of examples such as Brutus's 'If it be aught toward the general good,/ Set honour in one eye and death i'th'other,/ And I will look on both indifferently' (Julius Caesar, 1. 2. 85–7) and Coriolanus's 'I have done/ As you have done – that's what I can; induc'd/ As you have been – that's for my country' (Coriolanus 1. 9. 15–17), Cantor deduces that a 'sense of serving a cause larger than oneself is the cornerstone of Romanness in the Republic'. By contrast, when it comes to Shakespeare's imperial Romans, that is absent. For instance, when Antony speaks of 'the cause' (4. 9. 6), 'he means only that his soldiers should take his personal cause as his own' (Cantor, 38).

Strikingly, Cantor goes on to claim that, in Antony and Cleopatra, 'Not a word is spoken about the good of Rome in the course of the play: all one ever hears is the characters' concern for their relative positions in the pure struggle for power in the Empire' (Cantor, 38). The only statement that might be cited in support of the notion of a common good, he says, is the one made by Lepidus, who links it to the notion of political necessity and the prospect of war: ''Tis not a time/ For private stomaching' (2. 2. 8–9). But even that admonition is brought about by, and limited to, dealing with the immediate threat posed by Pompey. It is also, perhaps, precisely because of the indulgence in such 'private stomaching' on the part of most of his adversaries that, in the phrase of Thidias, Octavius is able to rise to the position of 'universal landlord' (3. 13. 72); or as Cleopatra describes him, with scarcely concealed irony, 'Sole sir o'the'world' (5. 2. 120). So, perhaps in ways that Antony had probably not contemplated him doing, Octavius nevertheless acted upon his advice, offered in connection with his drinking habits: 'Be a child o'th'time' (2. 7. 98).

'SHAKESPEARE'S ROMANS'

While the delineation of Octavius in the play is largely in line
with what is found in Plutarch and in Suetonius, what should be
noted is that the Octavius who would 'rather fast from all' is (at
the moment he utters the sentiment) not exactly sober: 'It's
monstrous labour when I wash my brain,/ 'An it grow fouler'.
(2. 7. 96–7). If Antony's immediate response (quoted a moment
ago) that he should be a child of his time might therefore be read
simply as advice to enjoy himself, it also points to the
recognition that Rome, with respect to matters of feasting, is
not that very different from Egypt. Recall that earlier, in
response to his host, Pompey's, observation that 'This is not
yet an Alexandrian feast', Antony who, on the evidence of
Plutarch's story of his carousings in Egypt (Bullough, 275–6),
presumably could be relied upon as a judge in that regard had
retorted: 'It ripens towards it' (2. 7. 93–4). What is at issue here is
not the extent of the speaker's inebriation, but why he should
feel the need to maintain his sense of self-image in the
circumstances in which he finds himself. Any comparison of
the relative states of Octavius and Lepidus, that 'third part of the
world', who is so drunk (2. 7. 89) that he has to be carried off by
a servant, must lead to the conclusion that inebriation is a matter
of degree, not principle. It is a misreading to cast Octavius in the
role of 'sober' politician. Cantor's summation is surely valid: 'It
is basic to Octavius's reluctance to drink... that he does not hold
his liquor well... Whatever airs he may put on in speaking of
"our graver business" (2. 7. 119), there is nothing high-minded
about his objections to indulgence. He is not, as some maintain,
a Stoic moralist condemning epicurean self-gratification. All
Octavius really objects to are the bad consequences of
indulgence' (Cantor, 29).

An equally pertinent example of taking Octavius at his self-
assessment is the scene in which he attempts to convey a sense
of his political philosophy:

> It hath been taught us from the primal state
> That he which is was wished until he were;
> And the ebbed man, ne'er loved till ne'er worth love,
> Comes deared by being lacked
>
> (1. 4. 41–4)

Note here the fastidiousness of the rejection of power that is dependent upon popular favour, as well as the distinction being made between the 'ebbed' and the 'deared', between those who are past it, who can only hold out the possibility of acquiring and dispensing the benefits that accrue from having power, and those who can offer actual and absolutist power – which Octavius holds out as the mark of the 'time of universal peace'. What is being asserted here is not some personal whim. Rather, Octavius's argument is that the theory he articulates had been the lesson taught since the 'primal state', that notionally first moment when human beings learnt to live in some sort of communal agreement. Once again Plutarch provides evidence of his political skill: when he had felt that his position (certainly vis-à-vis Antony) was still unsure, 'he himself sought the people's good will every manner of way, gathering together the old soldiers of the late deceased Caesar' (Bullough, 266). That was one way to deal with those whom Antony describes as 'Our slippery people,/ Whose love is never linked to the deserver/ Till his deserts are past' (1. 2. 184–6).

The most striking feature of Shakespeare's reworking of his material is that while he is largely faithful to sources, he from time to time rejigs those ever so slightly – to blisteringly damning effect. Octavius invariably tends to come out less favourably than he appears in the translations from the classics. We will see, later, that the reverse is true with regard to Antony, who comes out better in the play than in the sources. To demonstrate the case with reference to Octavius recall not only the episode on Pompey's galley, where Shakespeare alters the picture from that of an abstemious and thoughtful figure who, if not exactly the opposite of what he claims to be, certainly puts in question his assessment of himself. Not even his love for his half-sister, Octavia, can escape scrutiny. That his love for her and for her wellbeing is genuine cannot be doubted. Yet it is a love for her that he uses to his advantage. Against her insistence to the contrary, that he should not call her 'castaway' (3. 6. 40), he transforms her unheralded (in his view) return to Rome which 'prevented/ The ostentation of our love' (3. 6. 51–2) into the reason for dealing with Antony. And, at the end, notice how he, quite literally, wants to write himself into the record of history: he invites others to 'Go with me to my tent, where you

24

shall see/ How hardly I was drawn into this war,/ How calm and gentle I proceeded still/ In all my writings' (5. 1. 73–6). Small wonder that a politician for whom the written word was crucial should have been deeply offended by Antony's (mis)treatment of his letters: 'I wrote to you:/ When rioting in Alexandria you/ Did pocket up my letters, and with taunts/ Did gibe my missive out of audience' (2. 2. 75–8).

At issue here are not the acts, but the claims that these are constitutive of Roman 'honour'. To take one final, if obvious, example. For all his assurances to Cleopatra that 'We will extenuate rather than enforce./ If you apply yourself to our intents,/ Which towards you are most gentle, you shall find/ A benefit in this change' (5. 2. 125–8), we know, from what he had earlier told Proculeius: 'Go and say/ We purpose her no shame; give her what comforts/ The quality of her passion shall require,/ Lest in her greatness by some mortal stroke/ She do defeat us – *for her life in Rome/ Would be eternal in our triumph*' (5. 1. 61–6; my emphasis). But Cleopatra sees through him. Not only does she, famously, tell Charmian and Iras 'He words me, girls, he words me, that I should not/ Be noble to myself' (5. 2. 191–2), but earlier she had told him to his face about how she thought he saw those whom he had conquered and how they will be used – as 'Your scutcheons and your signs of conquest shall/ Hang in what place you please' (5. 2. 135–6). And then there are her almost last words, wholly dismissive of the new 'Sole sir o'th'world' (5. 2. 120) Those words note, are addressed to the asp, as part of her request to the 'Poor venomous fool' to 'Be angry, and dispatch': 'O, couldst thou speak,/ That I might hear thee call great Caesar "Ass/ Unpolicied!"' (5. 2. 304–7).

My reading of Octavius, as he appears in the text, is one which is in agreement with Cleopatra's justifiably contemptuous dismissal of him as 'ass unpolicied'. Michael Neill has glossed that phrase as 'political stratagems [which] have been brought to nothing; stripped of all his pretensions to political cunning' (Neill, 321). For David Bevington the phrase indicates Octavius being 'outmanoeuvred in the contest of "policy" or craft, including statecraft, for Cleopatra has foiled Caesar's ambitions' (to lead her in his Triumph in Rome).[15] The effect of such readings is the toppling of a dominant post-Second World War critical tradition according to which Octavius is elevated to the position not only of ideal (political) ruler, but also that of (moral) superior; especially when he is compared with the dissolute Antony: from which, by extension, the rightness of the succession to being 'sole sir o'th'world'. First made respectable by J. E. Phillips,[16] it was echoed by Maurice Charney: 'in Elizabethan histories and comparable works, the reputation of Octavius was very high; he was seen as the ideal Roman emperor, the restorer of peace, and the ruler of the fourth earthly monarchy'.[17] While Charney cites both Phillips and J. Leeds Barroll in support of his case, he does, nevertheless, hedge his bets by asserting that 'it would be more correct [what sort of convolution is that?] to say with Harold S. Wilson that Octavius "remains an enigmatic figure, implacable, menacing, cold, as the historical Octavius doubtless was; but a power rather than a person, a function of the developing action, the nemesis of Antony and Cleopatra, the tragic measure of their human limitation"'.[18] While Barroll[19] did, indeed, in 1958 have such a view of Octavius, by 1984 his praise is somewhat less fulsome: 'No matter how thoroughly we search, we never once detect Caesar in the performance of an act of generosity – it is not that Caesar is stingy, it is that he is wholly committed to the love of acquisition'.[20] It would be tedious to list the names of eminent Shakespeare scholars who have held the view, perhaps most succinctly expressed by Julian Markels[21] that 'Octavius is no villain but, like King Henry V, whom he so resembles in character, the agent of political order renewing itself'.

It ain't necessarily so! In Elizabethan stories dealing with Rome, the Octavius of the republic is seen as an ambitious nasty. William Fulbecke, for instance, makes it clear that, in his view, the reason why Rome had not reverted to a state of relative peace after the assassination of Julius Caesar could be found in the competing personal ambitions of the younger Pompey and of the man whom Caesar had designated his son and heir, Octavius: 'the commonweal did seem to have rolled herself into the state of her pristinate liberty, and it had returned unto the same, if either Pompey had not left sons, or Caesar had not made an heir'.[22] Fulbecke had questioned the right of Octavius to step into the place vacated by Caesar on the basis of law: that the honours conferred on the former were to the person, and could therefore not be transferable to the latter. A key issue for those who saw themselves as the heirs to Julius Caesar was the clearly unequal (in their view) inheritance. That was so, above all, for Pompey. It also explains why he behaves differently to each of the triumvirs. But while he is more friendly towards Antony than towards the others, he also makes clear the nature of his grievance: 'Thou dost o'ercount me of my father's house' (2. 6. 27). Here he makes use of the highly formal 'thou' towards someone with whom relations of obligation had been long-standing. As Plutarch has it, 'Sextus Pompeius had dealt very friendly with Antonius, for he had courteously received his mother, when she fled out of Italy with Fulvia: and therefore they thought good to make peace with him'.[23] That encounter includes not only his wounding depiction of Antony as a cuckoo; it ends with the prediction: 'But since the cuckoo builds not for himself,/ Remain in't as thou mayest' (2. 6. 28–9).

Yet, for all his sense of rectitude and probity in a world he sees as falling away from the Roman virtues espoused by his father, virtues for which he now sees himself as torch-bearer, the son's motives are not at all high-minded. The much-quoted rejection of the offer by Menas to get rid of the 'three world-sharers' by cutting the cable of the ship on which they are, and then their throats, is evidence, rather, that he would happily as well as willingly be the recipient of the benefits that would accrue, but would not be party to the deed:

> Ah, this thou shouldst have done,
> And not have spoke on't: in me 'tis villainy;
> In thee't had been good service. Thou must know,
> 'Tis not my profit that does led mine honour;
> Mine honour, it. Repent that e'er thy tongue
> Hath so betrayed thine act. Being done unknown,
> I should have found it afterwards well done,
> But must condemn it now

> (2. 7. 74–81)

It is difficult to see how an answer such as that can be construed as being that of a person of honour in the terms Rome saw itself by. Which might be one reason why the dramatist's borrowing here is somewhat more circumspect than what is in the source. As Plutarch has it, and Shakespeare faithfully restates, Pompey, 'having praised for a while upon it, at length answered him: "Thou should'st have done it, and never have told me, but now we must content us with what we have"'. What the dramatist leaves out is the very next sentence: 'As for myself, I was never taught to break my faith, nor to be counted a traitor' (Bullough, 279). But in this view of himself, Pompey miscalculates; as he does from the outset: 'If the great gods be just, they shall assist/ The deeds of justest men'. (2. 1. 1–2) And when Menecrates tries to warn him of the pitfalls – 'We, ignorant of ourselves,/ Beg often our own harms, which the wise powers/ Deny us for our good; so find we profit/ By losing of our prayers' (2. 1. 5–8) – he ignores the warning. He puts his trust, instead, in a combination of his highly proficient naval skills – but then misreads the intelligence brought to him. Not only will it transpire that his view that 'The people love me' and that his 'powers are crescent, and my auguring hope/ Says it will come to th'full' (2. 1. 9–11) will not be realized, but a moment later he will also be proven wrong in his belief that 'Mark Antony/ In Egypt sits at dinner, and will make/ No wars without doors' (2. 1. 11–12). It is a miscalculation that, in his relations with Antony, would prove fatal. Shakespeare merely hints at the story of Antony's part in Pompey's murder. Eros tells Enobarbus that his master is walking in the garden where he not only cries 'Fool Lepidus!', but also 'threats the throat of that his officer/ That murdered Pompey' (3. 5. 16–18). Michael Neill glosses that bit of information on the part of Eros as follows: 'By suppressing Anthony's involvement Shakespeare deliberately plays down the machiavellism of his historical original, while leaving the question of his possible complicity obscure' (Neill, 231).[24]

So, once again, Pompey's role is crucial in mediating the politics of the play. His death is deeply ironic on two counts. Firstly, that the person who requires an explanation from the triumvirate about the drenching of the Capitol in blood should (according to the story in Appian) violate a temple in honour of Juno. Bear in mind that that deity was, in Roman religion, not only wife and sister to Jupiter, protector of women and concerned especially with their sexual life; she later was to become the great goddess of the Roman state who is worshipped (with Jupiter and Minerva) at precisely that Capitol that was drenched with blood. Secondly, that he who had refused the offer made by Menas because of the condition upon which that offer was made ('Wilt thou be lord of all the world?') as well as the manner in which it was made, may perhaps have been the victim of an act made in the name of Antony by Plancus who 'had Antony's signet' and (according to one version) had acted in his leader's interests, but without that leader's knowledge or agreement.

And that story triggers off the story of the end of Lepidus. According to the account provided by Eros to Enobarbus: 'Caesar, having made use of him [Lepidus] in the wars 'gainst Pompey, presently denied him rivality, would not let him partake in the glory of the action, and, not resting here, accuses him of letters he had formerly wrote to Pompey; upon his own appeal seizes him – so the poor third is up, till death enlarge his confine' (3. 5. 6–11). It was, in a sense, an inevitable ending. The very first scene in which Octavius and Lepidus are shown together, in which they reflect upon the state of Rome as well as upon Antony's shortcomings, shows the relations of inequality between them. It ends in an exchange in which Lepidus has to beg/remind that he be included in the decision-making:

LEPIDUS   Farewell, my lord. What you shall know meantime
           Of stirs abroad, I shall beseech you, sir,
           To let me be partaker.
CAESAR   Doubt not, sir
           I knew it for my bond.

                                              (1. 4. 82–5)

It is, at first sight, an unexceptionable response on the part of Octavius: that he had always understood his obligations to the triumvirate. He will soon after accuse Antony directly: 'You have broken/ The article of your oath, which you shall never/ Have tongue to charge me with' (2. 2. 85–7). There is, however, scope for an alternative reading, argued as follows by Michael Neill: 'the cool tone of Caesar's reassurance is emphasized by the unexpected past tense, as well as by the slightly enigmatic way in which it is left hanging upon a half-line. The scene is already laying the ground for Caesar's casually announced coup against Lepidus'. (Neill, 173) The story of that coup is told with almost frightening economy. It is matched by the story told by Octavius, who informs Agrippa, without feeling the need to specify any details, that he had told Antony that 'Lepidus was grown too cruel' (3. 6. 32). Compare those stories, as found in

Plutarch and in Appian (Bullough, 291). In Plutarch, Octavius combines his explanation to the Senate with the story of how Antony had distributed imperial territories to Cleopatra and her children, and then goes on to say: 'that for Lepidus, he had indeed deposed him, and taken his part of the Empire from him, because he did overcruelly use of his authority'. The ironies are monumental: not only in the gall Octavius has of asserting that Lepidus 'was grown too cruel', but even more that he should be repaid in this way for his support of the judicial murder of Cicero, done at the instigation of Antony and eventually agreed to by Octavius.

The Antony encountered in the play is, as stated earlier, a heavily edited version of the one to be found in the translations. In the latter, two features, in particular, might be noticed. The first is that he apparently tended to behave in different ways towards the populaces of descent places: courteous in Greece; cruel in Asia; varied in manner towards the Romans – 'For he robbed noble men and gentle men of their goods, to give unto vile flatterers' (Bullough, 271–2). That image of Antony had long been in place in Rome, where 'the government of the triumvirate grew odious and hateful to the Romans, for divers respects. But they most blamed Antony, because he being older than Caesar [Octavius], and of more power and force than Lepidus, gave himself again to his former riot and excess, when he left to deal in the affairs of the commonwealth' (Bullough, 270). Plutarch is, nevertheless, at pains to show that Antony had 'singular gifts': 'Antony's nobility and ancient house, his eloquence, his plain nature, his liberalitie and magnificence, and his familiarity to sport and to be merry in company, but specially the care he took at that time to help, visit, and lament those that were sick and wounded, seeing every man to have that which was meet for him; that was of such force and effect as it made them that were sick and wounded to love him better, and were more desirous to do him service, than those who were whole and sound ... And stories circulated, not only of his military prowess, but also of his succour for his troops'. (Bullough, 259–60, 286).

Here the manner of Antony's treatment of Enobarbus is central – not only in itself, but also in comparison with the story of his treatment of Cicero. When he finds that Enobarbus has

30

deserted, he instructs Eros not only to send all his goods after him, but to write a letter he will sign of 'gentle adieus and greetings'; 'Say that I wish he never find more cause/ To change a master. O, my fortunes have/ Corrupted honest men' (4. 5. 14–17). And the soldier of Caesar's who brings news of the return of the treasure exclaims to an Enobarbus who says of himself that he is 'alone the villain of the earth' that Antony 'Your Emperor/ continues still a Jove' (4. 6. 29; 27–8). By contrast, Antony not only fought hard to get agreement to have Cicero executed, but that, having first had the body dismembered, 'when the murderers brought him Cicero's head and hands cut off, he beheld them a long time with great joy, and laughed heartily, and that oftentimes, for the great joy he felt. Then, when he had taken his pleasure of the sight of them he caused them to be set up in an open place, over the pulpit for Orations (where, when he was alive, he had often spoken to the people) as if he had the dead man hurt, and not blemished his own fortune, showing himself (to his great shame and infamie) a cruel man, and unworthy of the office and authority he bare' (Bullough, 269).

How to account for such actions on the part of a figure, Antony, whom, in the play, we are clearly expected to value – and rightly – over that of his rival Octavius? Although that is not the burden of her argument, Coppélia Kahn's close analysis of the relations between this 'pair of chaps' (3. 5. 12)[75] may well be one way into offering an explanation for the absence of a sense of organic unity in Rome·

> Antony and Caesar [Octavius] don't mirror each other as do Brutus and Cassius, fellow republicans, or Coriolanus and Aufidius, equally matched martial giants. Rather, their bonding is a specific instance of what Eve Kosofsky Sedgwick calls homosocial desire, 'the affective and social force, the glue, even when its manifestation is hostility or hatred or something less emotively charged, that shapes the relationship'.... Despite the obvious contrasts of character that distinguish Antony and Caesar, they mirror each other in blinding desire for *imperium*. This is 'the affective or social force, the glue' that binds them. Emulation binds them precisely because they are rivals for power, as Caesar's eulogy to Antony suggests:
>
> O Antony,
> I have followed thee to this; but we do lance
> Diseases in our bodies. I must perforce
> Have shown to thee such a declining day,

Or look on thine: we could not stall together
In the whole world.

(5. 1. 35–40)

This 'disease' is a cultural one, an agonistic style of interpellating men as rivals in an all-or-nothing contest.[26]

While arguments located in the consequences of competitive male relationships have much to commend them, what I hope to do later is to offer what the psychoanalytic misses out: an explanation for Antony's refusal to compete with Octavius in that 'blinding desire for *imperium*' in terms of a politics of response to colonial adventures on the part of the colonizer. Kahn's psychoanalytic and my postcolonial explanations will, I hope, be rather more tenable than the conventional crudities of a now outdated Marxist study (the author's claim, that, not mine) that is offered by Victor Kiernan, who says of Antony that

> He is adrift between two eras, and affords Shakespeare the opportunity for his most realistic, many-sided picture of a 'great man' phenomenon that always intrigued him –, but a man cashiered by history. Antony has dazzled the empire with remarkable qualities as a soldier and leader of men, if with little idea of where he was leading them; in the shipwreck of the republic, and a time of chaotic competition, he has found no worthy task to harness his energies to...His legacy is no tangible achievement such as Octavius will leave, but a revelation of human energy, courage and the power to love, even though he has destroyed himself by not knowing how to use these gifts.[27]

'THE TIME OF UNIVERSAL PEACE'

Much has been made of Octavius's prediction that 'The time of universal peace is near' (4. 6. 4). The remark should not be isolated from the rest of the speech: for two related reasons. Firstly, because of the qualification therein he himself makes about the foundations upon which that 'universal peace' will be built; secondly, because it provides an insight into the kind of self-fashioning history into which Octavius will write himself and later be written by historians of the Roman empire (notably by the Greek from Boeotia, Plutarch; also others like Appian, the Greek born in Alexandria) upon whose writings the dramatist would draw. 'Prove this a prosperous day, the three-nooked world/ Shall bear the olive freely' (4. 6. 5–6) is how Octavius concludes his prediction. While we can speculate about the precise meaning of the image 'the three-nooked world',[28] what is noteworthy is that the remark is made not only in the presence of the trusted Agrippa, but also in the hearing of the defector Enobarbus, who will soon after reveal the names of further defectors: notably Alexas and Camidius, and what happened to them.[29] Recall that Octavius makes his prediction in the play before Actium will have taken place. Thus, for the prophecy to be fulfilled it would have to be dependent upon Antony and Cleopatra being defeated. Peace, in the sense in which he means it, is possible only after the emergence of one single ruler. Peace only after judgement; though that, too, is qualified.

Even then there is a strong suspicion that the qualification is neatly managed to redound to the credit of one who will later be styled as Augustus. That suspicion, in turn, leads to another: what value to be placed on valedictions for the defeated: firstly, on Antony: 'The breaking of so great a thing should make/ A greater crack. The round world/ Should have shook lions into civil streets,/ And citizens to their dens. The death of Anthony/ Is not a single doom, in the name lay/ A moeity of the world' (5. 1. 14–19); secondly, on both: 'She shall be buried with her Antony – / No grave upon the earth shall clip in it/ A pair so famous' (5. 2. 356–8), finally, on the political significance: 'High events such as these/ Strike those that make them; and their story is/ No less in pity than his glory which/ Brought them to be lamented'/ (5. 2. 358–61). According to Michael Neill, Octavius's tribute to his dead rival is not only a fitting completion to 'the anticlimax of the hero's unheroic end'. It also, he goes on to say, 'flouts epideictic convention' (intended or serving to display oratorical skill; characterized by such a display), so that the effect is 'to register the victor's sense of slightly disdainful disappointment' (Neill, 77).

One question that arises is the extent to which the dramatist had intended a deliberate echo of that notion of a 'time of universal peace' in *Cymbeline* (probably performed in 1611). There, the king of an ancient Britain sees his kingdom as heir to the westward movement of empire, inherited from Rome, now made more cosmopolitan by the presence of Roman invaders, but bound together in a common enterprise.

> Publish we this peace
> To all our subjects. Set we forward, let
> A Roman and a British ensign wave
> Friendly together. So through Lud's town march,
> And in the temple of great Jupiter
> Our peace we ratify, seal it with feasts.
> Set on there. Never was a war did cease
> Ere bloody hands were washed, with such a peace.

(*Cymbeline*, 5. 6. 477–85)

The evocation of notions about 'all our subjects' and 'universal peace' pointing to shared sentiments on the part of the rulers (Octavius; James of England and Scotland; Cymbeline) takes us back to the question Pompey asks about the reason for the conspiracy against Caesar. Having earlier on drawn attention to the curt, perfunctory and calculatedly dismissive response from the triumvirs, in unison, 'Take your time' (2. 6. 23), as indication of their absolute refusal to engage with the question that is posed, it is needful to recall that the response to the last words of Julius Caesar as he dies from the stab-wounds: 'Et tu, Brutè? Then fall Caesar' is met with Cinna's 'Liberty! Freedom! Tyranny is dead! Run hence, proclaim, cry it about the streets' (*Julius Caesar*, 3. 1. 77–80).

If the assassination of Julius Caesar is symbol not only of the world of the rulers being turned upside down from within the ranks of the patrician class itself, it should also be recalled that one of the consequences of the assassination is that the unfranchised who populate the civil streets give effect to the new slogans by setting houses alight. Though some of those fires are doused by the creation of the triumvirate, they continue to spark insurrections and contests: by Fulvia and her brother; by Pompey; between members of the triumvirate. The only conclusion possible from itemizing events such as these, as well as others mentioned earlier, is that it is difficult to sustain the view of Rome as representative of stability and order. That conceded, it becomes difficult to go along with the view bruited abroad in Rome of Egypt, especially in the figure of Cleopatra, as a threat to that Roman stability and order. A similar problem arises when comparisons are made with the England of the history plays.

In the history plays it is the state and destiny of the English nation that is at issue. It is the contribution of individuals – Hal; Hotspur; Richard; Lord Scrope – as well as (by inference) groups, such as Welsh and Scots – that is the criterion for a judgement that might be said to suggest that the lives of individuals are subordinate to the general good of the nation. The examples are too numerous to mention; but obvious ones include the one by the self-styled 'prophet new inspired' John of Gaunt, whose valedictory paean of praise for 'This blessed plot, this earth, this realm, this England' also, we should remember, contains the regret that 'That England that was wont to conquer others/ Hath made a shameful conquest of itself' (*Richard II*, 2. 1. 50, 64–5); as well as the 'Cry "God for Harry! England and Saint George!"' speech before Harfleur and the Saint Crispian's day speech before Agincourt (*Henry V*, 3. 1. 1–34; 4. 3. 20–67). Judged by speeches such as those, one feature that distinguishes the histories as different from *Antony and Cleopatra* is that in the latter play not a single participant talks of Rome as shared community in the way that England is evoked in those histories. It is that distinction which perhaps explains why even Enobarbus, the one person who might have acted as choric commentator by invoking the common cause against Cleopatra as national cause does not do so. He leaves Antony because the latter has become 'so leaky/ That we must leave thee to thy sinking, for/ Thy dearest quit thee', (3. 13. 63–5). It is a distinction that also makes us aware that Pompey's challenge is not to be equated with the kind posed by (say) Hotspur. Limited and unequal as it certainly was, Henry IV's England could nevertheless legitimately lay claim to the existence of an organic unity that seems to me to be wholly absent in the Rome of the triumvirate.

Given the nature of the real relations (rather than that of the ordered *civitas* so beloved of some of the critics cited earlier) the actions of some of Antony's closest friends become, at least, explicable. The general thesis enunciated by Ventidius that 'A lower place, note well,/ May make too great an act. . . . Better to leave undone than by our deed/ Acquire too high a fame when him we serve's away./ . . . Who does i'th'wars more than his captain can/ Becomes his captain's captain; and ambition, / The soldier's virtue, rather makes choice of loss/ Than gain which darkens him' (3. 1. 12–24)[30] is arguably the most impressive instance of how *realpolitik* as practised in Rome is interpreted by those who carry out the wishes of their masters. The case of Enobarbus is rather more complex. He, too, in his moment of decision, formulates a phrase that rivals that of Ventidius's notion of his 'captain's captain'. When he finds that 'Mine honesty and I begin to square', he comes to the conclusion that 'he that can endure/ To follow with allegiance a fall'n lord/ Does conquer him that did his master conquer/ And earns a place i'th'story' (3. 13. 41–6). After all, his earlier intervention in the exchanges between members of the triumvirate had met with a rebuke: not from Octavius, but from his master. The choice of language is noteworthy. The response to his prediction that if Octavius and Antony 'borrow one another's love for the instant, you may, when you hear no more words of Pompey, return it again. You shall have time to wrangle in when you have nothing else to do', is met by his leader and friend reminding him, 'Thou art a soldier only: speak no more'. It is that pulling of rank on the part of those who have it and can choose to use it when it pleases them to do so that prompts in Enobarbus the recognition about the real relations that mark Rome's politics: 'That Truth should be silent, I had almost forgot' (2. 2. 108–13).

What is clear in the play – and an inheritance from its predecessor – is precisely the absence of any evidence to justify any interpretation of 'Rome' as a political practice worthy of emulation. As the most celebrated scourge of the Roman legions in the last village in Gaul that has not been subdued, Asterix, so often reminds us: 'These Romans are crazy!' Which phrase has been memorably and appropriately translated from the original French into Italian as '*sono pazzi questi Romani*' (SPQR: *Senatus Populusque Romanus* – Senate and People of Rome).[31]

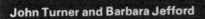

John Turner and Barbara Jefford

3. Antony and Cleopatra from the 1977 Prospect Theatre production at the Old Vic, London.

4. Antony and Cleopatra from the 1978 RSC production, Stratford-upon-Avon.

4

Egypt:
'A lass unparalleled'

INTRODUCTION

Probably no other female figure in a Shakespeare play is vilified
to the extent that Cleopatra is. She is abused with a variety of
epithets which, no matter how poetically these are sometimes
expressed, in the end, nevertheless, come down to one simple
assertion: that the Queen of Egypt is a whore! It is a view
expressed in the first place by those Romans who hold her
responsible for their claim, for which Philo is spokesperson, that
Antony's 'captain's heart,/ Which in the scuffles of great fights
hath burst/ The buckle of his breast, reneges all temper,/ And is
become the bellows and the fan/ To cool a gypsy's lust' (1. 1. 6–
10). Though he rapidly recants, it is an accusation made by
Antony as well, when he comes to the realization that he has lost
the military – and therefore the political – contest with Octavius.
Flailing around for reasons for his defeat, he echoes the view
that Cleopatra, 'Like a right gypsy hath at fast and loose/
Beguiled me to the very heart of loss' (4. 13. 28–9).

It is not, of course, the first time in a Shakespeare play that
Cleopatra is likened unto a 'gypsy'. Mercutio, predicting to
Benvolio that a disconsolate Romeo might probably resort to
writing sonnets on the Petrarchan model, goes on to add that:
'Laura to his lady was a kitchen wench/...Dido a dowdy,
Cleopatra a gypsy, Helen and Hero hildings and harlots' (*Romeo
and Juliet*, 2. 3. 35–7). Note that while the speakers are,
respectively, Roman and Veronese, the sentiments being
expressed are English and stem from contemporary perceptions of, and attitudes towards, those referred to as 'gypsies'.

Despite the fact that English people of those times had neither direct nor reliable knowledge about Egypt, such absence of knowledge did not stop them from ascribing national, as well as 'racial' characteristics to those they so designated: thievery; cunning; whoredom; harlotry; but also skill in dancing. One of the most influential statements was the following, from which may have arisen the notion of Egyptians – and therefore, of Cleopatra, as black ('swarte'): Andrew Borde's 1550 description: 'Egypt is a country joined to Jewry./ The country is plentiful of wine, corn, and honey./ ... The people of the country be swarte and doth go about disguised in their apparel. Contrary to other nations they are light-fingered and use piking. They have little manners and evil longing and yet they are pleasant dancers. There are few or none of the Egyptians who dwell in Egypt now, for Egypt is repleted now with infidel aliens. Their money is brass and gold'.[1]

If the phrase 'infidel aliens' for Early Modern English readers conjured up the image of the Ottoman empire at the time of its greatest power and influence under the rule of Suleiman the Magnificent (1494–1566; Sultan 1520–66), of which Egypt was then a part, official attitudes to gypsies at home were to be found in legislation of considerable severity enacted by English parliaments: imprisonment and forfeiture of goods (2 Henry VIII, 1530); raised to that of a felon's death for 'Egyptians and other persons commonly called Egyptians' (Mary I, 1554). Popular opinion was also influenced by the output of pamphlet literature[2] against the phenomenon of 'masterless men'[3] (some of whom were popularly referred to as 'gypsies'), who roamed the English countryside in a period marked by 'enclosures' – the conversion of the hitherto common fields into private property – with the result that large numbers of people were thrown off the land – though, as witnessed by the example of Robert Kett in Norfolk in 1549, they sometimes rebelled.

Pompey's epithet, 'salt Cleopatra', with the speaker's own lascivious injunction to the absent queen that she should 'soften thy waned lip! ' (2. 1. 21), echoes that notion of the lustful female Other. He hopes that 'our stirring' (his challenge to the triumvirate) 'Can from the lap of Egypt's widow pluck/ The ne'er lust-wearied Anthony' (2. 1. 37–8). The lip-smacking voyeurism of the language continues in Agrippa's 'Royal wench', with the first word referring to the status of Queen of Egypt and the second pointing to that of women of the lowest social status. That oxymoron, in its turn, prompts recollection of the story of Cleopatra's meeting with Julius Caesar, expressed in a blunt no-nonsense combination of the military and the agricultural: 'She made great Caesar lay his sword to bed,/ He ploughed her, and she cropped'. (2. 2. 234–5). It is a phallic image of ploughing which Bevington notes is as old as the first Chorus in the *Antigone* of Sophocles. One other comes to mind: the story of the 5th-century BCE Roman Cincinnatus who was on two separate occasions forced to leave his farm to defend the city (first to defeat the invading Aequi; next, the revolting plebeians). After each, he chose to return to his farm rather than participate in running the state. He it was who is reputed to have been an early coiner of a version of the idea of turning swords into ploughshares; of making love, not war.

Agrippa's sentiments have no such high-minded intent. His observation is sandwiched in between two extended commentaries by Enobarbus: the first, in the famous evocation of the queen on her barge (2. 2. 198ff); the second, the reason why Antony would not leave her (2. 2. 242–7). But what might appear, at first sight, as evidence of admiration and approbation can, nevertheless, be read as having an opposite intent. With regard to the first, Catherine Belsey has drawn attention to the most remarkable feature of the 'barge' speech: that 'Cleopatra is not present in the account of her appearance in the barge, whether as a person or as a body'.[4] The second statement, that the 'vilest things become her', seems to be there in order to provide evidence for the assertion that the holy (though clearly not Christian) priests bless her when she is at her most 'riggish' (licentious). It is a remarkable feat of sophisticated abuse masquerading as praise. And, from a Roman point of view, not without reason. Each one of the key participants (either directly, or through the agency of their supporters) needs to set up Cleopatra, in advance of the possibility that it might happen, as scapegoat for their failures.

It is that side of her as 'whore', as described by Enobarbus, that Pompey hopes will prevent the 'ne'er lust-wearied Antony' from rejoining the two other triumvirs. His chances of success in the confrontation will be greatly assisted by Antony not being a participant. And not for the first time. While still in Egypt, Enobarbus had responded to Antony's unconvincing observation that he 'must from this enchanting queen break off' (1. 2. 128) with three remarkably revealing comments: (a) in a language of sexual bawdy that associated death with orgasm; which latter act, according to Roman gossip, it would appear, Cleopatra managed swiftly, as well as often: that 'Cleopatra catching but the least noise of this [expression of the desire on Antony's part to leave her] dies instantly' (1. 2. 139–40); (b) that while her tears and sighs are real, she also has a highly developed cunning (skill) to counterfeit. The alternative, clearly unacceptable explanation would be to concede that her skills would be on a par with that of Jove, since her 'passions are made of nothing but the finest part of pure love. We cannot call her winds and waters sighs and tears; they are greater storms and tempests than almanacs can report. This cannot be cunning in her; if it be, she makes a shower of rain as well as Jove' (1. 2. 145–50); (c) what at first sight might appear to be praise turns out to be the opposite. To Antony's 'Would I had never seen her!', the response is that he 'had then left unseen a wonderful piece of work, which not to have been blest withal, would have discredited your travel' (1. 2. 151–4). Enobarbus is, according to Bevington 'probably invoking a satiric literary tradition at the expense of contemporary fashion for travel and the notoriety of extravagant travellers' tales'.[5] Small wonder then that, not soon after, when Menas responds to the prophecy by Enobarbus that the 'bond that seems to tie' the friendship between Antony and Octavius 'will be the very strangler of their amity' (because 'Octavia is of a holy, cold, and still conversation') with the remark 'Who would not have his wife so?', Enobarbus can, with confidence, assert that 'He [Antony] will to his Egyptian dish again' (2. 6. 119–21, 123, 125.) Octavia's sighs are not only very different from those of Cleopatra; they are inferior: her 'conversation' will not 'die' with 'celerity'.

But Enobarbus, as it turns out, is mistaken in his prognostication about the role that Octavius's half-sister will play. Octavia will try hard to act as mediatrix between the two antagonists. That her return to Rome will be used as an excuse to 'blow the fire up in Caesar' (2. 6. 126) is not of her making: neither in the play, nor in the sources Shakespeare consulted. Still, when

Octavius welcomes his 'most wrongèd sister' (3. 6. 65), resolutely refusing to concede that hers was an amicable departure from Athens and from Antony, Maecenas can take it upon himself not only to assert that 'Each heart in Rome does love and pity you' (3. 6. 93), but can then proceed to put all blame on 'th'adulterous Antony' who had given 'his potent regiment to a trull/ That noises it against us'. (3. 6. 96–7) My sense is that while an audience might go along with the 'adulterous' part and have sympathy for Octavia in that regard, they would also recognize that she is being used by her brother, and have sympathy for her in that as well.

What is noticeable about Antony's statements to Cleopatra, as well as about her, is how his remarks are apparently shaped by their contexts: which is a feature of his decision-making generally. Unlike Octavius, who is shown as having thought out various strategies in advance, Antony does not give the impression that he makes decisions until such time as he is forced into doing so. Here, his opening construction of Cleopatra as 'wrangling Queen', with its sense of her as quarrelsome, is immediately qualified by the recognition that 'to chide, to laugh,/ To weep – how every passion fully strives/ To make itself in thee fair and admired!' (1. 1. 50–53) is evidence of his admiration of her moods. The remark can also be read as evidence of 'wrangling' (now in an older usage of the word, that of disputation in a university) that she will seem the fool she knows she is not, but that 'Anthony/ Will be himself'. His response, 'But stirred by Cleopatra' (1. 1. 44–5), is surely evidence, right from the outset, and in direct opposition of the view of her enunciated by Philo to Demetrius, of Cleopatra's perspicacity.

Antony's portrayal of Cleopatra as being 'cunning past man's thought' (1. 2. 144) not only shows once again how he 'will be himself'; it also shows that his practice is to blame others – in this case Cleopatra – for his shortcomings. It is a habit of his to which attention is drawn again soon after, when Octavius will accuse him: 'You praise yourself/ By laying defects of judgement to me' (2. 2. 58–9). He might call her, as Cleopatra tells Mardian, his 'serpent of old Nile' (1. 5. 25); but for fear that 'You'll heat my blood. No more!', he refuses her request to 'play one scene/ Of excellent dissembling, and let it look/ Like perfect honour'

41

(1. 3. 80; 78–80). Then, having returned to Rome, he sends Mardian back with an 'orient pearl' and a speech in which he instructs the eunuch to tell Cleopatra that 'All the East/... shall call her mistress' (1. 5. 46–7). It was that promise made by Antony to Cleopatra, reported here to Agrippa and Maecenas, that Octavius used in a speech to the Senate in order to persuade that body to declare war on her (3. 6. 1–11; 13–18).

Predictions of the great future, relayed by a messenger, will not prevent Antony from calling her other names to her face. Coming upon the sight of Thidias kissing her hand, he calls her 'kite' (3. 13. 89). Once again she is metamorphosed into bird of prey, whore. Indeed, not soon after, he accuses her of having 'been a boggler ever' (3. 13. 111). Furthermore, as evidence of his by now deep sense of victimhood, he postulates a theory for exculpating himself. Instead he advances the theory that 'the wise gods seel our eyes' (3. 13. 113), that is, hoodwink (cover up the eyes, as is done with falcons trained for the hunt) so that those to whom that is done, like him, can 'make us/ Adore our errors, laugh at's while we strut/ To our confusion' (3. 13. 114–16). From there, he proceeds to throw her past in her face – with a quite formidable venom: 'I found you as a morsel, cold upon/ Dead Caesar's trencher – nay, you were a fragment/ of Gneius Pompey's'[6] (3. 13. 117–19). Still, he speedily snaps out of his accusatory mood, blaming it upon the sight of Thidias being 'familiar with/ My playfellow, your hand' (3. 13. 125–6). He pleads with her, apologizes to her as nearly as he can – 'Where hast thou been, my heart?' – and promises that 'If from the field I shall return once more/ To kiss these lips, I will appear in blood; / I and my sword will earn our chronicle –/ There's hope in't yet' (3. 13. 173; 174–7).

When he does return from the battle, Cleopatra is, for a moment, restored as 'this great fairy' (4. 9. 12), the repository of magical gifts, to whom Antony will commend the heroic acts accomplished by Scarrus. But, recall that it was that soldier who had earlier referred to the queen as 'Yon ribanded nag of Egypt –/ Whom leprosy o'ertake! ' (3. 10. 10–11). Michael Neill[7] sees the phrase as referring to Cleopatra's beflagged ship on which Enobarbus had commented before the battle of Actium, as well as to the gaudy costume of some over-dressed whore. No wonder that the promise to the 'great fairy' becomes transformed into the charge that 'This foul Egyptian has betrayèd me' (4. 13. 10), that she can now be described as a 'Triple-turned whore!' (4. 13. 13) who had 'sold' Antony to the 'novice' Octavius, and who, upon entering upon the scene, is cried out against: 'Ah, thou spell! Avaunt!' (4. 13. 30). Even taking into account the special and longstanding animus between the two triumvirs, there is surely some validity in the advice Octavius proffers Thidias: 'Observe how Antony becomes his flaw' (3. 12. 35); meaning, presumably, not only how his flaws are a mark of his personality, but also the manner of his behaviour in the face of adversity: invariably, he blames others as the cause of his failures. But such railings are soon spent; perhaps most famously in the scene after the defeat at Actium, where he asks her 'O whither hast thou led me, Egypt', with the result that he would now 'To the young man send humble treaties' (3. 11. 50, 61), he can switch moods as well as words. To Cleopatra's 'Pardon, pardon!', his response is 'Fall not a tear, I say.../ Give me a kiss – Even this repays me' (3. 11. 67–70). Finally, Bradley's view of Antony's 'generous and expansive nature', quoted earlier, can be sustained from remarks made by Cleopatra's eulogy: 'His legs bestrid the ocean...', notably for her view that 'For his bounty/ There was no winter in't' (5. 2. 82ff).

It is salutary to compare Charmian's valediction for her mistress, addressed to Death, in whose possession now 'lies/ A lass unparalleled' (5. 2. 314–15) with the lies, alas, unparalleled that have been spoken about her, as well as to her, by the Romans. To those lies the queen's responses have tended to show remarkable forbearance, as well as wisdom. Thus, when Antony attempts to explain why he has to return to Rome, the soaring poetry of her 'Eternity was in our lips and eyes,/ Bliss in our brows bent; none our parts so poor,/ But was a race of heaven' is sandwiched between two quite straightforward and matter-of-fact lines: 'Nay, pray you seek no colour for your going,/ But bid farewell and go' and 'thou, the greatest soldier of the world,/ Art turned the greatest liar' – from which follows the conclusion, 'I would I had thy inches, thou shouldst know/ There was a heart in Egypt' (1. 3. 35–41). Those critics who stress Cleopatra's 'See where he is, who's with him, what he does:/ I did not send you' (1. 3. 2–3) instruction to her women as evidence of so-called 'feminine wiles', it seems to me, either deliberately misread or wittingly refuse to credit her always mature recognition of the political ramifications that drive Antony's departure. For instance, Charmian's advice that she 'In each thing give him way, cross him in nothing' is met not only with the firm reprimand, 'Thou teachest like a fool', but also with evidence of her recognition of the consequences that would follow from such a policy: that is 'the way to lose him' (1. 3. 9–10). The point I seek to make is simple. Her critics may not like what she does, or how she does it. What they cannot continue to get away with is to go on denying the political dimensions for decisions she makes. Furthermore, not only does she invariably offer explanations for such actions on her part; they also tend to make sense.

To take the instance of her striking the messenger who brings the news of the marriage of Antony and Octavia. Critics intent on making her a harridan appear not to have noticed the messenger's protest: 'Gracious madam,/ I that do bring the news made not the match' (2. 5. 67–8), itself an echo of the comment made earlier by the messenger who had brought Antony the news of Fulvia's death: 'The nature of bad news infects the teller' (1. 2. 95). While the messenger's 'gracious madam' could be dismissed as convention, the fact that he observes the niceties even after 'she hales him up and down' is worthy of note. Critics ignore two even more important features of the encounter: (a) Cleopatra's fulsome apologies about the incident; (b) the political theory that she enunciates. With regard to the first, not only does she volunteer to her women that 'These hands do lack nobility that they strike/ A meaner than myself, since I myself/ Have given myself the cause' (2. 5. 83–5), but when the messenger asks her 'Should I lie, madam?', her answer is unequivocal: 'O, I would thou didst' (2. 5. 94), since 'Though it be honest, it is never good/ To bring bad news' (2. 5. 86–7); and especially so because it is Antony's 'fault should make a knave of thee,/ That act not what thou'rt sure of' (2. 5. 103–4).

Neill, as well as Bevington, draw attention to the problem this line has caused editors. The former suggests that it might mean either 'you who are after all innocent of this offence that you know about' or 'you who are unable even to convey the news'. Bevington offers the more convoluted gloss that 'it's regrettable that Antony's fault should make you a villain in my eyes, you who are not yourself hateful like the fact you're so sure of'. As I see it (and without wishing to simplify), the answer lies in Cleopatra's earlier admonition to the messenger about the dangers attendant upon being the bearer of bad news. That observation, as well as her subsequent actions of striking the messenger and then apologizing for it, spring from a theory she enunciates even before she strikes: 'some innocents scape not the thunderbolt!' (2. 5. 78) – a remarkably apposite thesis, not only for the politics of the play, but also for Elizabethan and Jacobean political theory generally. That it is a remark given to Cleopatra, rather than to any of the more 'politic' Romans must have been done with deliberate intent: as counterpoint to Rome's denigration of her as whore. But then, the queen is not only self-aware; she is also willing to take responsibility for her own actions. Refusing to see herself as the 'triple-turned whore' that Antony calls her, in his rage, she thinks of that past he throws in her face with affection as 'My salad days,/ When I was green in judgement' (1. 5. 73–4).

Above all, that awareness of the political dimension to her actions is manifested in the message she sends to Octavius via Proculeius. It must have been galling for him to have received a message to the effect that, in her view, his accession to the position of 'Sole sir o'th'world' (5. 2. 120), as he undoubtedly had become, was because she had sent him 'the greatness he had got'; especially since she had made it abundantly clear, a few moments before, that ' 'Tis paltry to be Caesar –/ Not being Fortune, he's but Fortune's knave' (5. 2. 2–3).

CRITICISM'S KNAVES, AND THEIR 'OTHERS'

Recognition of Cleopatra's sense of self as expressed in the play raises the question of the extent to which the playwright has deliberately set up a dramatic situation that invites the audience not simply to wonder about the reason for the abuse, but also specifically to reject the accusations made by the Romans, and (until recently) repeated by some of the most eminent Shakespeare scholars of the last hundred years. The core of my argument is that even when some of these eminent men (and the odd woman) of the past praise her, those praises are feigned. For them Cleopatra continues to be the exotic, the courtesan, the Other. Noteworthy is the excess they import into the reading of the dramatic text. So too is the tenacity with which such representations persist into the present.

To take one recent example against which to stake out my own position with reference to the matter of Self and Other. For Linda Bamber[8] there are three Cleopatras: (a) the embodiment of Egypt and a symbol of 'our' (undefined by Bamber but presentably female) experience; (b) representative of the Other as against Antony's representation of the Self; (c) the Cleopatra who, like Antony, facing failure and defeat, is motivated by the desire to contain or rise above her losses. None of these versions of Cleopatra, for Bamber, quite reach the heights that mark the 'tragic hero' – notably a feature she identifies as 'moments of dissatisfied self-scrutiny', evidence of which she finds in Lear on the heath, condemning himself for forgetting the poor (*King Lear* 3. 4. 29–34); Othello despairing of himself after killing Desdemona (*Othello*, 5. 2. 283–8), and Antony accusing himself of cowardice after hearing news of Cleopatra's suicide.

But views along such lines have also been massively modified. Although her tale is structured mostly around the histories, Phyllis Rackin is surely right in stating that 'The protagonists of Shakespeare's history plays, conceived both as subjects and as writers of history, were inevitably male. The women who do appear are typically defined as opponents and subverters of the historical and historiographic enterprise – in short – as anti-historians. But Shakespeare does give them a voice – a voice that challenges the logocentric, masculine historical record'.[9] Rackin here quotes Linda Woodbridge, who (as Linda Fitz) had asserted that 'Women's tongues are instruments of aggression or self-defense; men's are the tools of authority. In either case speech is an expression of authority; but male speech represents legitimate authority, while female speech attempts to usurp authority or rebel against it'.[10] Uncomfortably aware of the ironies of my situation in the context of the above, I would, nevertheless, wish to add one further – and, to me, central – feature about the matter of Self and Other, with reference to Cleopatra. Against the generally accepted notion of Cleopatra as 'Other' contra Antony's representation as Self, as most critics have tended to see the matter, my assertion is a simple one: It is not *Cleopatra who is the Other. It is the others who are Others to her!*

46

'ENLIGHTENMENT' SHADOWS

Two particular shadows of a tradition of literary criticism since the Enlightenment which continue into the present are those of terminologies of sexism and racism. With reference to the first, it is Schlegel's formulation (1811) that defines the terrain and sets the tone: 'The seductive arts of Cleopatra are in no respect veiled over; she is an ambiguous being made up of royal pride, female vanity, luxury, inconstancy, and true attachment. Although the mutual passion of herself and Antony is without moral dignity, it still excites our sympathy as an unsurmountable fascination: – they seem formed for each other, and Cleopatra is as remarkable for her seductive charm as Antony is for his deeds'. For the German critic the point of it all is simple: that of the male figure 'always shipwrecked against the seductions of an artful woman. It is Hercules in the chains of Omphale, drawn from the fabulous heroic ages in history, and invested with the Roman costume'.[11] Cleopatra, like Omphale, is figured as dis-membering masculinity.

For William Hazlitt (1817) Cleopatra is 'voluptuous, ostentatious, conscious, boastful of her charms, haughty, tyrannical, fickle...Cleopatra's whole character is the triumph of the voluptuous, of the love of pleasure and the power of giving it, over every other consideration'. What 'almost redeems' her 'great and unpardonable faults', for Hazlitt, is the 'grandeur of her death', in which moment 'She keeps her queen-like state in the last disgrace, and her sense of the pleasure in the last moments of her life. She tastes a luxury in death'.[12] Strange, the transfer here. 'Voluptuousness' is a weakness of character Octavius ascribes to Antony, who 'filled/ His vacancy with his voluptuousness' (1. 4. 25–6). And while it is not at all easy to decode what Hazlitt might have meant, what should be noted is the confidence of the sentences he pronounces: that her 'faults' are 'unpardonable' – even though she is 'almost' redeemed despite her 'last disgrace'. Even her royal status is reduced to that of a 'queen-like state'.

One possible consequence of views such as these is that when Cleopatra is perceived as having finally 'conquered' her 'passions', the credit for that is given to Antony. Thus Thomas MacAlindon (1973) claims that 'Her constancy is studied and

47

involves a determination to acquire Antony's masculine virtues...' The very strength of Cleopatra's grief – her perception of how weighty her loss has been – helps her to become a queen over her passion...Her final change...is from levity to gravity, from weakness into unchanging nobility, from bondage to liberty, from concubine to wife, from becoming into being'.[13] Or, in other words, coming into 'being' involves becoming a (becoming?) wife. Though not even then! For Schücking (1919) 'the essential vulgarity of her character is also shown by the pride which, like every courtesan, she takes in having had so many distinguished lovers'[14] while for Leo Kirschbaum 'the obvious harlot' is 'still, however transformed, the same courtesan – avid of love, impatient, jealous of rivals, quick-tempered, voluptuous, feline, thinking in sheerly female terms'.[15] While it is tempting to speculate about the experiential basis for the confidence with which some male critics can call her harlot, it is perhaps safer to point out that what Kirschbaum is doing is to take issue with Swinburne (1879) and G. Wilson Knight (1931), both of whom had seen her as 'eternal woman'[16] – though one who also, above all, happens to be, and remains, an Egyptian, therefore alien, Oriental, not quite 'one of us'.

How can someone who is then an amalgam of the 'eternal [European?] feminine' and Egyptian 'wiles', be taken seriously? After all, no less a critic than the distinguished Marxist, Victor Kiernan, can assert that

> Court business in Alexandria is little more than a chase after amusements. Cleopatra has never acquired, what Antony has been losing, a serious interest in government: power means to her only royal trappings...Her prank of hopping forty paces through a street suggests a regime grown light-hearted, playing the mountebank. There is all the same something endearing in the thought of an unconventional queen strolling about her city, close to her people in this manner at least...The Cleopatra of the final scene can never have thought of handing over her lover to his enemies, as some allege. She may have thought of running away again, as she did from the seafight....She may be "cunning past man's thought"...but only in the short-sighted wisdom of her own courtesan lore...Like Lady Macbeth she ruins the man she loves, and herself with him. Cleopatra, however, does not lure Antony into crime, only into weakness.[17]

The symbol of that weakness is Actium, and the queen's role in that defeat figured as 'cowardice', as 'betrayal'. For E. A. J. Honigmann (1976), Actium is only the first of five consecutive 'betrayals'. For that critic, her first plea to 'Forgive my fearful sails' (3. 11. 54), and the kiss between them that is supposed to seal his agreement, solves nothing. Indeed, for Honigmann, her 'betrayal' is compounded in the scene (3. 13) in which she allows Thidias to kiss her hand. The third example, which, according to Honigmann, 'presents Cleopatra even more damagingly as a betrayer' has to do with the events after the sea-fight (4. 13). While he recognizes MacCallum's view that Cleopatra could in no way be held responsible for her fleet's 'treachery', his case is that since Antony believes it to be so, therefore it is so. And even though Honigmann concedes that MacCallum might well be right in pointing out Cleopatra's question 'Why is my lord enraged against his love?' (4. 13. 31) to be genuinely one of surprise, he dismisses that as 'posing'. How, after all, he asks, can she fail to know the answer to her own question? For him it therefore comes as no surprise that the fourth 'betrayal' is that Antony is convinced that she had 'Packed cards with Caesar' (4. 15. 19). But, he goes on to say that, good chap that Antony is, the minute he finds out that she is dead, 'he discards his former suspicions and forgives her'.

If the Roman triumvir is here rather more magnanimous than the British critic, the latter still blithely pursues his quest until he can find evidence of a fifth (and final) betrayal: 'before long, he [Antony] hears, too late, that she still lives, and has therefore betrayed him once more'.[18] Is it a naive response to point out that since, in each of the five cases (as Honigmann himself admits), it is Antony who is responsible for the conclusions he reaches, it is Antony who might perhaps be held responsible for his beliefs; that it is simply perverse to hold Cleopatra responsible for Antony's misreadings, hence inappropriate decisions about what to do next.

The problem is that Honigmann is not alone. For H. W. Fawkner, what we have here is an instance not of 'a desertion intensified by another, but a pursuit of a deserter'[19] – a designation to be taken up again in the final chapter. Yet Cleopatra's justification for participation in the battle could not have been clearer:

> Sink Rome, and their tongues rot
> That speak against us! A charge we bear i'th'war,
> And as the president of my kingdom will
> Appear there for a man. Speak not against it,
> I will not stay behind
>
> (3. 7. 15–19)

Compare the marginalization of Cleopatra's speech in comparison with the celebration of the speech that Elizabeth made to her troops at Tilbury, especially for her reputed remark: 'I have the body of a weak and feeble woman, but I have the heart and stomach of a king, and of a king of England too, and I think foul scorn that Parma or Spain, or any prince of Europe, should dare to invade the borders of my realm; to which, rather than any dishonour should grow by me, I myself will take up arms'.[20]

GENDER: OMPHALE AND HERCULES

Cleopatra and her closest associates not only remember these events differently; they also tell a different set of stories about them. The obvious context in which to read those is that of gender, defined by Catherine Belsey as follows in her Preface to the series Gender, Culture, Difference:

> Gender attends to the power relations inscribed in the areas patriarchal history treats as incidental: sexuality, private life and personal relations, cultural difference itself. At the same time it also recognizes transgression of the existing conventions as a mode of resistance, and therefore takes an interest in behaviour traditionally classified as perverse or dangerous. Above all, it is able to identify the differences within the relationships and practices it explores, treating them not as unified and homogeneous, but as contradictory to the degree that they participate in the uncertainties, incoherences, and instabilities of the cultures where they are found.

Here arguably the most brilliant is Cleopatra's clearly fondly remembered telling of how 'next morn,/ Ere the ninth hour, I drunk him to his bed –/ Then put my tires and mantles on him, whilst/ I wore his sword Philippan' (2. 5. 20–23). Bear in mind that this story of transgression of the conventions comes not only immediately before the event in which she strikes the messenger, but, even more importantly, immediately after brief dialogue, first

50

with Charmian, next with Mardian. Invited by the queen to play a game of billiards with her to while away the time, Charmian declines, pleading soreness in her arm, and suggests Mardian as alternative. Cleopatra's response 'As well a woman with an eunuch played,/ As with a woman' is followed by the invitation, in the form of a question 'Come, you'll play with me, sir?' That elicits the response 'As well as I can' (2. 5. 5–7).

Not only are these exchanges knowingly sexual, with their bawdy references to 'good will' even when that 'will' comes 'too short', but the queen's remarks culminate in the assertion that under such conditions the actor (presumably whether performing on stage, or in bed) 'may plead pardon' for coming so short (or perhaps so short a coming?). What Mardian may well be too polite to articulate is that the inability to perform does not rule out desire: after all, when, at an earlier moment, the queen had absolved him because he was 'unseminared' (castrated), his response was not only that he had 'affections', but that those affections were 'fierce' ones when he thought of 'What Venus did with Mars' (1. 5. 17–18).

Since a game of billiards is not possible, she will, instead, to the river to fish, where, as she draws up the 'Tawny-fine fishes', she will 'think them every one an Anthony,/ And say "Ah, ha! You're caught"'. It is that observation which triggers in Charmian the recollection of an earlier expedition in which the queen's 'diver/ Did hang a salt fish on his [Antony's] hook which he/ With fervency drew up' (2. 5. 12–18).

What audiences might not have known (but which critics certainly should) is that Shakespeare had here neatly selected one aspect of the tale, as told in Plutarch. According to that story, because Antony had on a previous occasion failed to catch any fish, he had 'commanded the fishermen that when he cast in his line they should straight dive under the water and put a fish on his hook which they had taken before'. According to Plutarch, Cleopatra 'found it [the deception] straight, and when Antony was unsuccessful the next time, retaliated by getting one of her men to dive under the water and hang a salt fish (not normally found in rivers) on his hook. Having all had a good laugh, Cleopatra's advice was "Leave us, my lord, Egyptians, which dwell in the country of Pharus and Canobus, your angling rod. This is not thy profession. Thou must hunt after conquering of

51

realms and countries"'.[21] It is a general thesis about his comparative lack of success in water that Antony will ignore, to his cost, later, instead insisting on 'By sea, by sea' (3. 7. 34–40).

It is Charmian's recollection of that moment of substitution of a 'salt' fish at the riverside that sparks Cleopatra's recollection of the much more talked about substitution of 'tires and mantles' and 'sword Philippan'. The first redirects Pompey's epithet 'Salt Cleopatra' (2. 1. 21) back at the Romans while the second points to the possibility that Antony had sought to hide from her his rather novel method of catching fish in order to impress her, but she made it clear to him, not only that she had been aware of his attempts at substitution, but also what she was doing in response: her transparently playful effort makes a deliberate mockery of his possibly intentionally deceitful behaviour. It is vivid reminder of a remark she had made at the beginning of the play: that she knows that he is incapable, even when asked to do so, of playing 'one scene/ of excellent dissembling' (1. 3. 78–9); but that she, for her part, will 'seem the fool I am not; Anthony/ Will be himself' (1. 1. 44–5).

As, it would seem, had been the case with Hercules (the figure whom Antony had claimed as ancestor[22]) who had fallen in love with Omphale, Queen of Lydia, to whom he agreed to be sold in expiation of the crimes of murdering a guest and of desecrating the abode of Apollo at Delphi. In the play there are several references to the claims Antony had made for the connection. The effect of every one of these is to his disadvantage. Cleopatra, very near the beginning, and famously, tells Charmian to 'Look.../ How this Herculean Roman does become/ The carriage of his chafe' (1. 3. 83–5). Then, when soldiers on guard in Antony's camp hear 'Music i'th'air' as well as 'Under the earth', one observes that '''Tis the god Hercules, whom Antony loved,/ Now leaves him' (4. 3. 14–15). This is, in itself, an interesting and clearly deliberate emendation on the part of the playwright, since in Plutarch the music being played is sign that it is Bacchus, god of music as well as of wine and of fertility, who leaves him.

Later, still, in the speech in which Antony claims that 'To the young Roman boy [Octavius] she hath sold me', he concludes that 'The shirt of Nessus is upon me' (4. 13. 48, 43) – a reference to the myth that when Hercules (or 'Alcides, thou mine ancestor', as Antony calls him here) had killed the centaur Nessus with a poisoned arrow because it had attempted to rape Hercules's wife Deianira, the dying Nessus had given his shirt, soaked with the poisoned blood, as a supposed love-charm for her husband. When Hercules put it on, the poison so maddened the wearer that, in his dying rage, he flung Lichas, the servant who had brought the shirt, into the sea. Versions of the Hercules story, notably those via the medium of translations from works attributed to Seneca were, according to H. B. Lathrop,[23] in popular circulation from the 1580s. According to Lucy Hughes-Hallett: 'The legend was frequently referred to in Greek and Roman literature as the prototype of a relationship within which a woman had subjugated a man. Roxanne was said to have played Omphale to the Hercules of Alexander the Great. Pericles's mistress Aspasia was known as "the new Omphale"...The comparison was a commonplace of the Roman propaganda directed against Cleopatra'.[24] Anne Barton is surely right in her observation that 'Certainly there is something not just unattractive but maimed about the exclusively masculine world of Rome in this play'.[25]

That masculine world gets its come-uppance in Cleopatra's death. She wants that event to be 'after the high Roman fashion,/ And make death proud to take us' (4. 16. 88–9). That desire should be placed in the context of the manner of Antony's final moments. Despite his admission to the guards that 'I have done my work ill, friends' (4. 15. 105), he revises that view to assert that he dies 'a Roman, by a Roman/ Valiantly vanquished' (4. 16. 59–60). The contest goes right to the end. And with a quite remarkable upshot. As John Drakakis has argued, from what would seem to me to be impeccably psychoanalytic paradigms allied to an equally firmly grounded sense of historical specificity, Cleopatra's

> death is a parody which mocks Caesarism even as it imitates Roman values. It is a death which imitates sleep, a prelude to a marriage which parodies through exaggeration of Roman institutions. Its fantasy of a transcendentally 'comic' exposes the desire for an inclusive harmony and the possibility of its realization in the imaginary realm of the theatre. Within this 'wooden 0' the opposition is not between the 'real' (Egypt) and the ideological (Rome), but between different fantasies of the 'real'. Egypt may well

be the space where Roman values are parodied, and subverted, but it is also the place where they are sustained. Similarly, Egypt may be the space where Roman cynicism can find its full expression: 'No grave upon the earth shall clip in it/ A pair so famous' (5. 2. 357–8), but its fecund venality continues to exert its attraction. In its alternation between comic and tragic endings, the play discloses the constitutive power of particular fantasies, which are, by definition, inseparable from the realm of politics.[26]

It is to one very important fantasy, inseparable from the realm of politics, that of Cleopatra's colour, that I now turn.

CLEOPATRA'S 'BLACKNESS'

The constitutive fantasies constructed by dominantly male (and mostly white) critics of Cleopatra as a whore who also threatens patriarchy, can be said to have been comprehensively dismantled by recent studies – notably from within the ranks of cultural materialist and feminist theorists. One new feature that has sprung from those rewritings has been an interest in what is commonly referred to as 'Cleopatra's color'; itself a kind of shorthand for a congeries of terms remarkable for the instability of their meanings: 'colour' itself, and 'black' or 'blackness' in particular as essential elements in the discourses of 'race'. What should be constantly kept in mind is how some of those terms were shaped in determinate historical moments: the Rome of the classical writers; the Early Modern England of the text; the Europe of the Enlightenment, later exported to the rest of the world as a key element of the imperial imposition. Now, in a moment that is referred to as 'postmodernist' and 'postcolonial', one key feature that marks the discourses is the input from critics whose ancestors were those 'others' who found themselves inscribed in the texts about first contacts. While much of this re-excavation of the foundations has led to really quite brilliant remapping of the terrain, this quite obviously long (often deliberately bypassed) endeavour has also resulted in some quite egregious outcomes. Examples from some recent attempts to find in Cleopatra a 'role model' provide evidence across the whole range of the spectrum of this process.

For Janet Adelman (1973), 'it is slightly alarming that criticism has not speculated more widely about the issue of Cleopatra's color, particularly since directors have to make these decisions for every production';[27] for Ania Loomba (1989), Renaissance politics and stagecraft shaped Cleopatra as 'the non-European, the outsider, the white man's ultimate "other"';[28] for Kim Hall (1995), 'Shakespeare's *Antony and Cleopatra* is the play that perhaps is most closely concerned with the ways in which an African queen threatens empire. Cleopatra's darkness [sic] makes her the embodiment of an absolute correspondence between fears of racial and gender difference and the threat they pose to imperialism';[29] for Joyce Green MacDonald (1996) 'As a woman and a "blacke" woman at that, Cleopatra and her impromptu mythography signify all the more powerfully because of the scarcity of black women in early modern representations of race'.[30]

Noteworthy in these statements is the difference between them. Adelman does not claim that, in her view, Cleopatra has a black skin; she hedges her bets: 'Cleopatra tells us that she is black [1. 5. 28]; but her use of the word is by no means clear' (Adelman, 84). But then, neither are those used by the critic. She is spot on when she claims that 'when Shakespeare wants us to consider race as an issue, he makes the point abundantly clear: that there is no mistaking it in *Titus Andronicus* and *Othello*': except that her terminology reveals that she here falls into the common trap of using the deeply problematic category of 'race' (which she never defines) anachronistically as synonym for skin colour. To claim, as she does, that 'There is nonetheless reason to suspect that Shakespeare imagined Cleopatra as dark; her darkness is traditionally part of her mystery' and that 'gypsy' was the popular name given to 'tawnyskinned nomads, originally of Hindu stock, who began to wander about English lanes and commons early in the sixteenth century, and were supposed to come from Egypt', she is right about the nomenclature being used, but mistaken about the 'racial' as well as the geographical origins. Notwithstanding, she is right to remind that 'despite geographical confusions, Egypt and Africa did not carry interchangeable associations in the Renaissance; though both were foreign, they belong to different traditions... most writers in the Renaissance assume that Egypt,

55

not Ethiopia, first found out letters, arts and science: Africans were generally assumed to be backward in culture, but Egypt was the birthplace of civilization itself' which leads her to conclude that 'Cleopatra's tawniness contributes to the sense of her ancient and mysterious sexuality, whether or not she is an African; to Shakespeare's audience, what probably mattered is that she was darker than they were' (Adelman, 188). But then, why such an opening gambit that expresses 'alarm', when all that the endgame reveals is that Cleopatra's skin was darker than that of her audience?

Ania Loomba's interrogation of the issue is splendidly sophisticated. Not only is her argument that 'The figure of Cleopatra is the most celebrated stereotype of the goddess and whore and has been accommodated and shaped by centuries of myth-making and fantasy surrounding the historical figure'; she also gives reasons for unravelling 'the several different strands of contemporary meaning which intertwine with connotations attaching to her [Cleopatra] from earlier stories'. For Loomba, 'Shakespeare does not simply indicate a stereotype but depicts it as constructed by various male perspectives in play'. Later, she will argue that 'such a construction is then challenged and dismantled'. In the process of her argument, Loomba offers five ways in which 'Renaissance politics and stagecraft shape Cleopatra's presentation'. It is important to headline each of these, not simply because they offer a brilliant summary of several of the positions I have tried to state, at various times, in this monograph, but because the order in which Loomba gives them is significant for the particular issue – that of Cleopatra's colour – being discussed here.

Firstly, 'the construction of Cleopatra draws upon the medieval notion of the sexual appetite of women as rampant and potentially criminal'; *secondly*, 'Cleopatra's social position places her in a contradictory position. Status, wealth, class are refracted in their operation through the prism of gender, and do not work the same way as for men'; *thirdly*, 'the idea of Cleopatra's dichotomous identity is elaborated in the images of her play-acting, dressing up, putting on disguises, planning and stage-managing her encounters with both Antony and Caesar. She is the supreme *actress* – theatrical, unruly and anarchic, whose "infinite variety" also derives from the roles she plays';

fourthly, 'Cleopatra's play-acting specifically reverses gender roles' (Loomba, 75–8). Only fifthly comes the Renaissance construction of Cleopatra as 'the non-European, the outsider, the white man's ultimate "other"'. Save for the quibble that it is to be doubted that it is possible to use the term 'class' with reference to the Early Modern period (as Loomba does in her second point), her argument seems to me to be unexceptionable. For our purposes, what should be noted is her (correct) introduction of the term 'non-European'; here as well as in her more recent work on Shakespeare and cultural difference[31] I also read this as her not making the claim that Cleopatra is either 'black' or 'African'. It is to the politics and the stagecraft of the Renaissance that we can trace the assumption.

For Kim Hall,

> race, as much as class, becomes a crucial category used by women writers to differentiate between female characters.
>
> The representation of Cleopatra in women's texts of the early modern period clearly displays the nexus of beauty, race, and empire in such differentiation between women. Cleopatra's sexual allure seems as problematic as her political/erotic power is compelling. Unlike most male writers, women writers continually remind their readers of Cleopatra's dark foreignness.

which feature, Hall asserts, is because 'it is precisely this disjunction between Cleopatra's reputation for beauty and her (dark) foreignness that would be intriguing to European women because it offers a space from which to negotiate an otherwise confining system of beauty'. As evidence for what is clearly an important feature, Hall mentions, among other writers, Aemilia Lanyer, who in her *Salve Deus Rex Judaeorum* (1611) emphasizes 'the blackness of the adulterous Cleopatra along with her beauty'. Hall claims that 'there seems to be an emerging female tradition of a dark Cleopatra' (Hall, 182–3, 155).[32]

On the evidence she provides, the argument remains unproven. Indeed, Hall's arguments tend to be generalized rather than particular. For instance, the assertion that 'Racial otherness allows white men to lump all "others" (male and female) into another less valued group. In the devaluing of dark-haired women as "Ethiops" or "Tartars", all people of color are placed in secondary positions that reinforce European hegemony' (Hall, 182). Perhaps so; but how is that evidenced in the case of this particular text? Above all, it seems to me that Hall herself stops short of making the claim that Cleopatra was 'black'. Furthermore, while Early Modern writers did, indeed, in the confidence of their ignorance, confuse and sometimes equate 'Ethiops' and 'Tartars' (sic), care should be taken, in the present, not to reduce them to that really rather offensive locution 'people of color': the Tatars are (and were) largely Turkic-speaking peoples living in parts of the former Soviet Union as well as in East Central Asia; their skin colour covers the whole spectrum of varieties of 'white'. In *The Merchant of Venice*, the Duke appeals to the 'Jew' to act not to 'press a royal merchant down' as was to be expected 'From stubborn Turks and Tartars never trained/ To offices of tender courtesy.' (*Merchant of Venice*, 4. 1. 28, 31–2). And Henry, in explaining to the traitor Richard, Earl of Cambridge, why 'The mercy that was quick in us but late,/ By your own counsel is suppressed and killed', states that it is for fear that 'that same demon that hath gulled thee thus/ Should with his lion's gait walk the whole world,/ He might return to vast Tartar back/ And tell the legions, "I can never win/ A soul so easy as that Englishman's"' (*Henry V*, 2. 2. 76–7, 118–22).

Whereas 'Tartars' are associated with mercilessness, the feature that marks 'Ethiops' is, indeed, the fact of their blackness; often physical manifestation of evil. Looking at the handwriting on the letter Silvius offers her, Rosalind proclaims 'Women's gentle brain/ Could not drop forth such giant-crude invention,/ Such Ethiop's words, blacker in their effect/ Than in their countenance' (*As You Like It*, 4. 3. 33–6). But not invariably. For instance, in *Pericles*, Thaisa explains to her father that the first knight who presents himself at the tournament is from Sparta, 'And the device he bears upon his shield/ Is a black Ethiop reaching at the sun. The word, *Lux tua vita mihi*' (*Pericles*, scene 6, ll. 19–21). 'Your light is my life', written on his shield, is here clearly an association very different from that of the more familiar and often-quoted remark by Lysander to Hermia: 'Away, you Ethiope!' (*Midsummer Night's Dream*, 3. 2. 258). Since she is the daughter of Egeus, Duke of Athens, there must be a reasonable presumption that she is literally not! Why should it be assumed, on equally flimsy grounds in the text and against the grain, that Cleopatra is black?[33]

As far as can be ascertained, the only critic who argues that she is black is Joyce Green MacDonald. Indeed, for that critic, not only is Cleopatra black, but her 'impromptu mythography signify all the more powerfully because of the scarcity of black women in early modern representations of race'. But such ascriptions, as MacDonald herself admits, will work only 'if we accept this Cleopatra's reference to her dark skin as literal, the way in which she explains its origins does indeed race as well as gender her subjectivity in ways which depart from the traditional portrayals of those other North African queens in whose company I believe, along with Neill, she properly belongs' (MacDonald, 61). Now, first of all, I doubt that Neill's story supports MacDonald's. For Neill, Cleopatra's 'radical otherness'

> is registered in both cultural and gender terms by a [Roman] world which defines its own "virtue", conceived as masculine, self-restrained, and rational, against an "Eastern" voluptuousness, imagined as feminine, histrionic, capricious, and dangerously fecund. Such oppositions have been read as expressing the play's uncomplicated endorsement of racialist and sexist essentialism *However, we have only to put Cleopatra's playful sense of herself as "with Phoebus' amorous pinches black"* [1. 5. 28] *alongside Othello's anguished "haply for I am black"* [Othello, 3. 3. 267] *to recognize how relatively insignificant ... is the issue of racial difference in Antony and Cleopatra* (Neil, 87); my emphasis).

Neill is surely right, instead, to insist that it is gender that 'is foregrounded throughout, and systematically associated with cultural difference'. In any case, is it too simplistic a reading to suggest that what Cleopatra means by her being 'with Phoebus' amorous pinches black' (1. 5. 28) is that, in Antony's absence, the only caresses she gets are from the sun! A reading such as the one I have just offered might be regarded as making the playwright out to be having an elaborate joke at those who refer to the queen as 'tawny'. In our own time, and especially since the publication of Martin Bernal's *Black Athena*[34] the question of the queen's 'blackness' has taken on a particular stridency in North American debates that have as much to do with current dis-contents than with past de-nigrations.[35]

I should also wish to question MacDonald's view of Cleopatra as 'an African' and radically reposition what I think she means but does not spell out about Cleopatra as 'a queen determined to establish and maintain herself in power' (MacDonald, 62). Not only is it clear from the examples and citations that MacDonald herself adduces, that classical, as well as Early Modern writers, tended to differentiate between 'Egypt' and 'Africa', but the post-1970s usage of the term 'African' is dominantly North American in origin. Part of that story can be traced to responses to institutional racism in the United States (and, indeed, in Britain). Indeed, such excavations and reformulations of the African pasts tend to date from the moment of the colonial slave trade, which meant that the contacts were mainly with West Africa and (in the case of English experience) after Shakespeare's time. To say that is not to 'absolve' him; rather it is to raise the matter of what might legitimately be expected to be found in texts of the period that rely so much on classical sources and travellers' tales that, in their time, were taken to be accurate.[36] The European view of the world that MacDonald, as well as Hall, describes comes much later. It dates from the late seventeenth and early eighteenth century, a time marked by a shift away from classical notions of diversity on which difference was founded, to notions of absolute and unchanging principles, upon which difference was re-invented in radically different ways. And it should be remembered that even those new inscriptions were challenged in those very moments of their invention.[37] Our own time is, in some of those respects, not much different. One of the political outcomes of localized readings such as those developed in the United States since the 1970s is that they are exported to, and imposed upon, those spaces from which they are claim to have originated.[38]

As to the second, the queen, whose political skill is (as MacDonald quite rightly states) present in Shakespeare's text, sought to maintain herself in power. She could be described, making use of current terminologies, not as an Egyptian, but as a 'colonialist', the European oppressor. Cleopatra was a Ptolemy, descendant of one of the generals of Alexander the Great of Macedon, who had overrun Egypt in 332 BCE and whose rule lasted until replaced by another group of foreign masters, the Romans, who took over in 30 BCE and who themselves ruled until 395 CE; and who were, in their turn, replaced when Egypt became part of the Byzantine empire (395 CE to 638 CE). Being of Macedonian origin and part of the Ptolemy clan that practised

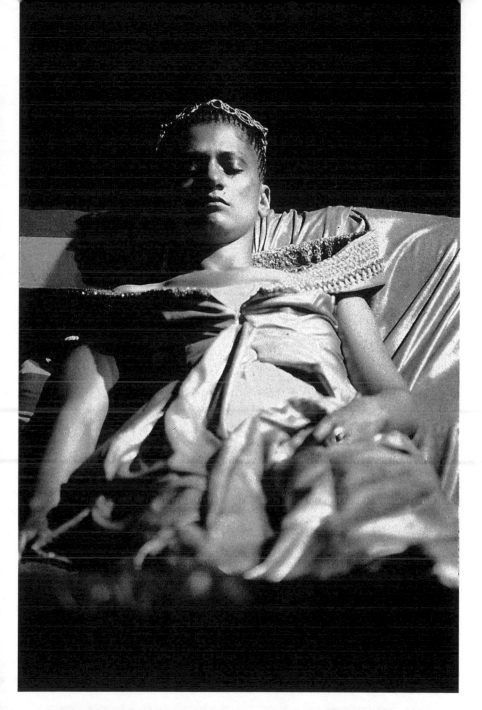

5. Cleopatra's death scene (Act 5, scene 2), from the 1998 English Stage Company production at the Hackney Empire, London.

6. Cleopatra's death scene (Act 5, scene 2), from the 1987 [Royal] National Theatre, London production.

intermarriage even between close siblings, she was almost certainly white. Wholly sympathetic to the responses to the politics of racism and sexism which drive the desire for affiliation and identification, I am, nevertheless, bound to rewrite Mark Twain: 'Reports of Cleopatra's blackness are greatly exaggerated'.[40]

5

Conclusion: 'Past the size of dreaming'

THE CENTURY OF THE PTOLEMIES

To describe the rulers of Egypt at the time of some of the events being enacted in *Antony and Cleopatra* as 'colonialists' and 'oppressors' is not only anachronistic, it is also misleading. To do so is to impose upon political relations in antiquity terminologies which, in our time, evoke images of European conquerors and their 'Others' in Africa, Asia and the Americas during the past five centuries. And yet: to describe the Ptolemies as 'oppressors' might not be wholly inaccurate. For Elizabethan and Jacobean readers it is highly likely that their first, and primary, association with 'Egypt' was that it was the place upon which God inflicted plagues in order to force the Pharaoh to allow Moses to lead the Israelites out of their bondage there (Exodus 3–12). Furthermore, from their reading of the translations from the classical chroniclers they would have chiefly been aware of two details about Cleopatra, both of them having to do with the Jews.

In a period when, formally and legally, Jews were forbidden to live in England, readers of the translations would have discovered that, early in her reign, when the Nile failed and there was the threat of famine, Cleopatra had given orders to open the granaries in order to feed the Egyptian people; but had deliberately forbidden that grain be given to the Jews who lived in Alexandria: by the letter of the law, they were not citizens. Secondly, readers would have been aware of her desire to be ruler over the lands which had once been part of the Ptolemaic empire but over which Herod now ruled. What is

62

important about this second example is that it offers an insight into her political skills. It was in order to achieve that objective that she enlisted Antony. It also influenced the nature of the deal she subsequently made with Herod. Her decisions were, therefore, in many ways, as hard-nosed as any of those made by Octavius. Herod, who had earlier been driven from his lands by the Parthians, and had been able to return only because Antony, as overlord of the East had used military powers to reinstall him, was forced to give up to Cleopatra the highly profitable plantations of balsam trees and date palms near Jericho. She then swiftly and skilfully leased back those plantations to their former owners and compounded that business deal by two further sophisticated and tough details: (a) she forced Herod to pay rent to her for the use of the land; (b) she also required him to collect on her behalf the taxes owed to her by other minor rulers in the region. It was political practice of a kind that Elizabeth might have been proud of.

Then there was also the story that in 36 BCE, when Antony had gone off to wage his eventually unsuccessful war against the Parthians, Cleopatra had returned to Alexandria via Jerusalem. While in Jerusalem, she reputedly tried to tempt Herod into some sort of sexual liaison about which (it is reputed) she could later complain to Antony, and thus create a rift between the two men, at a time when Herod was a committed supporter of the Roman. Since Herod, too, was one of the rulers who later deserted Antony for Octavius, the story in Josephus that his response to Cleopatra's overtures was to escort her 'with all the honour due to her' as far as the border might either be interpreted at face value, or as an effort on Herod's part to place whatever relations he had with Cleopatra in a light most advantageous to his needs. The point of retelling stories such as these is because it was actions of this kind that begin to account for the animus shown against her in the accounts by Josephus. I suppose that, for Josephus, she was (to make use of contemporary parlance) anti-Semitic.

In the play these events are brilliantly highlighted in two brief moments. (a) When Alexas observes that 'Herod of Jewry dare not look upon you', her response is: 'That Herod's head/ I'll have'. When asked how she would manage that, she not only explains how she would do it, but why it was not then possible:

'but how, when Anthony is gone,/ Through whom I might command it?' (3. 3. 3. 5–6); (b) there is the little episode of one of Charmian's wishes: 'let me have a child at fifty, to whom Herod of Jewry may do homage' (1. 2. 28–9). Both of these stories would have had clear biblical resonances. While writers and readers of the time were not always scrupulous in distinguishing one from another, with regard to the first instance, readers would have made an immediate connection with the story in the Bible of the presentation of the head of John the Baptist by Salome to Herod Antipas, son of Herod the Great who was Cleopatra's antagonist. It is that Herod the Great, best known for being responsible for the Massacre of the Innocents (Matthew 2: 16) that Charmian has in mind: presumably a child at 50 would have been as immaculate a conception for those times as a virgin birth!

Cleopatra was a Ptolemy, a direct descendant of Ptolemy I Soter ('Saviour'), one of the generals of Alexander who conferred upon himself the royal title (305 BCE) after the death of the Macedonian conqueror of Egypt (311 BCE). The Ptolemies, like the Persian overlords of Egypt before them, tended to respect local religion and customs and indeed sought to present themselves as legitimate heirs of the Pharaohs. Alexander had travelled (331 BCE) to the Temple of Amun, where he was greeted by the high priests as the son of that sun god, Amun-Ra. Then, when, in the first year of her reign, the sacred bull Buchis, which was worshipped as the living soul of Amun died, Cleopatra and her brother not only went to Upper Egypt for the installation of the new bull; they were also part of the escort of the vessel that made the crossing with the animal to its new home.

Some of these Ptolemaic rulers of Egypt, notably Ptolemy III Euergetes ('Benefactor'), were briefly successful in creating their own empires in Asia Minor. His successor, Ptolemy IV ('Father-Lover'; 222–204 BCE), however, inaugurated a period of mismanagement of the state marked by successive generations of family strife after power, military failures, and (from time to time) rebellion. Indeed, it was one such rebellion that resulted in Cleopatra's father, Ptolemy Neos Dionysos (81–51 BCE) being expelled by his daughter, Berenice. His restoration (55 BCE) was made possible only because of Roman support. The familiar name 'Flute-Player' assigned to Cleopatra's father is a reasonable (and presumably not intended to be flattering) indication of what, according to the chroniclers, the Egyptians thought of him. By the time Cleopatra was born (69 BCE) the writ of the Ptolemies has declined to embrace only the central regions and the city of Alexandria. In the Mediterranean world, Syria had become a Roman province in 64 BCE; Asia Minor was administered either by governors sent out from Rome, or by petty satraps who pledge allegiance to it. Indeed, two decades later, powerful Macedonia would itself become a mere province of Rome.

As in Egypt, so, too, in Rome. Extension of the imperial reach into other regions of Europe, Asia Minor and North Africa took place side by side with political instability at home – marked, as indicated earlier, by events such as the challenge of Pompey the Great; the assassination of Julius Caesar; the battle of Philippi; eventually the accession to being 'sole sir o'th'world' by Octavius. Rome, as I have shown, was not the stable and ordered place of historical and literary criticism of the nineteenth and twentieth centuries. The title page of Appian's chronicle made the nature of the real relations of power in Roman times, and the lessons to be drawn from it in Early Modern times, abundantly clear – especially that the reason for the first meeting between Julius Caesar (then aged 52) and Cleopatra (then aged 21) described by Enobarbus as 'A certain queen to Caesar in a mattress' (2. 6. 71) was not in order for them to go to bed with each other, but in order for him to enlist her support in sorting out the problems created by her brother, ruling as Ptolemy XIII, who had arranged for the killing of Pompey the Great who had sought refuge in Egypt after his defeat at Pharsalus.

According to Plutarch, what clearly impressed Julius Caesar was Cleopatra's facility with languages – her only aide was the Sicilian, Apollodorus, who had carried her to him wrapped in the mattress. Then there was her political bargaining skill. Indeed, one interpretation of Julius Caesar summoning her to Rome (where she lived between September 46 BCE and April 44 BCE) was in order to have her out of Egypt while he made preparations for his wars in the East. In Rome, he proclaimed her 'Friend and Ally of the Roman People', and had a golden statue of her set up near the temple built in honour of Venus Genetrix, reputedly the founder mother of the Julii, and therefore the divine ancestor of his line. In doing so, Julius

65

Caesar made a declaration that was not only an expression of personal love, but one that had enormous symbolic significance, in Egypt as well as in Rome, since the Ptolemies (male, as well as female) had, for generations, been regarded as temple-companions of the gods. Furthermore, while in Rome, her house was a centre for political and philosophical talk to which even Cicero had come. It was only after the death of Julius Caesar that the philosopher's dislike for her surfaced. But that might also be explained by his sense of hurt at having been sidelined in Roman politics by Caesar – for which, once again, Cleopatra got the blame.

Given the constant shifting of the political allegiances that were often expressed by means of military exploits, so brilliantly expressed in the Ventidius theory about the dangers of becoming 'his captain's captain' (3. 1. 22), it is possible to propose that what Cleopatra sought to do, throughout, was to secure the (by her time, much-reduced in size) Ptolemaic empire, as well as to win some of it back. There were practical and economic as well as political reasons for that. For instance, the recovery of parts of the lands rich in reserves of seasoned timber would enable the enlargement of the Egyptian fleet and the chance to restore Egypt as a strong sea-power; particularly desirable now, given the way in which Pompey's pirates were operating at sea.

One powerful sign of Cleopatra's intentions was in the propagandistic naming of the twins she had with Antony. They were called Alexander and Cleopatra Selene. The name for the boy conjured up the memory of the founder figure; the second names of both children linked them to astrological speculations about the dawn of a new Golden Age for Egypt. When the third child was born, he was named Ptolemy Philadelphus, in memory of Ptolemy II, ruler of Egypt in the years of its greatest power and importance. In order to achieve her objectives, she made it clear that she was aware that she required the assistance of a strong Roman – brilliantly captured in Cleopatra's explanation to Alexas about how she would set about having 'That Herod's head' (3. 3. 4). For Rome, the evidence of the success of the queen's policy of expansion of her own imperial designs, aided by a Roman, was the 'donations' made by Antony to the queen and to her children, vividly expressed by Octavius to Agrippa and Maecenas (3. 6. 1–10, 13–18), referred to in the preceding chapter. All of which was true. Indeed, not only did Cleopatra appear in public dressed as Isis (even carrying the golden rattle with which that goddess was associated) but coins depicting her were struck. Furthermore, a cult along these lines spread to Rome itself and apparently grew to so great an extent (or was perceived to be doing so) that the Senate tried, on five separate occasions between 59 BCE and 48 BCE to suppress it. Whether or not due to the strength of the adherence to that cult that developed, the Senate was forced, in 43 BCE, to agree that a temple to Isis be erected in Rome.

While Octavius spread the story that was to be highlighted in the play, namely that Antony had given away 'Roman' lands because he had become the 'the bellows and the fan/ To cool a gypsy's lust' (1. 1. 9–10), what is clear is that these decisions were the outcomes of political choices. Cleopatra had her own vision of territorial aggrandizement. She also recognized that her power to achieve any of her goals depended upon Antony's support and goodwill. Even though Egypt was a vassal state of Rome, it was more important than others because of two key differences from the others: (a) it was the granary of the empire; (b) it was strategically central to all military activity in the empire in the East. Whereas, in the West, the empire was administered directly by governors sent out by Rome, who were protected by Roman garrisons, the situation in the East was completely different. Roman policy there emphasized that the burden of administration and defence should be passed on to rulers of the client states. Even that was not new. When Pompey the Great was in charge, he had formed a cordon made up of such vassal states that stretched from the Black Sea, across Asia Minor, all the way to the borders of Arabia. Antony's dealings with Cleopatra, as with Herod, were a continuation of that policy.

The reason for Antony's eventual failure, according to Plutarch, had very little to do with Cleopatra's supposed hold over him. The first, and most important, was a strategic blunder, the failure to invade Italy in the summer of 32 BCE, when Octavius was having his problems at home because he had antagonized the landowners by imposition of punitive new taxes to pay for his wars. Despite appeals to him to return,

Antony instead made his headquarters at Athens. This decision sent all the wrong signals to Rome. Athens was the place where he had earlier made his home with Octavia, until he evicted her. It was also the city in which, for more than a century, there had been a festival dedicated to the Ptolemaic dynasty. Now, it was bruited abroad in Rome that the new ruler of that Egyptian dynasty would herself come to Athens. For Cleopatra to be in Athens would be a slap in the face for Octavia, and also for Rome, where it was further suggested that the reason why Antony had forced Octavia to leave was because Cleopatra had issued him with an ultimatum to do so. The fact that Octavia refused to blame her husband, and indeed defended him to her brother, not only made Romans rally to her side; it also lost Antony friends where he needed them most: in Rome itself. Perhaps most poignantly, Octavius escaped punishment for violating the sanctity of the temple protected by the Vestal Virgins, because, when he demanded from them the will and testament that Antony had left in their charge, Roman anger at his violation of the temple was exceeded by their anger at the news of what was contained in Antony's will. When Octavius revealed the details (the main terms of which were recognition of Caesarion as Caesar's legitimate son and that Antony's body be buried in Alexandria) the decision of the Senate – brilliantly orchestrated by Octavius – was to declare war. Not against Antony: that would have been tantamount to admission that what was afoot was civil war. Crucially important, war was declared against Cleopatra alone!

'CHRONIC DESERTER'

For Ernest Schanzer (1963), Antony is a 'chronic deserter'. He does, however, qualify his accusation of cowardice in the face of a unnamed enemy: 'I feel sure it would be a gross falsification of Shakespeare's conception to see Antony in these changes as a conscious deceiver, hiding his true feelings from Caesar, Octavia, or Cleopatra. Rather should we see him as sincere in all his protestations, believing each to be true at the moment it is uttered, until he is suddenly drawn into a contrary alliance'.[1] Schanzer does not tell his readers why, in his estimation, it would be 'a gross falsification of Shakespeare's conception' to see Antony as a 'conscious deceiver'. The play does indeed provide several instances of the fluctuations in Antony's mind – his response to the death of Fulvia: 'What our contempts doth often hurl from us,/ We wish it ours again; the present pleasure,/ By revolution low'ring, does become/ The opposite of itself' (1. 2. 123–6).

Some critics see the response as personal, rather than political. Their explanations tend to become highly convoluted. Janet Adelman (1973) puzzles about the key relationships by asking three questions: Why did Antony marry Octavia if he planned to return to Cleopatra? Was Octavius ruthless or merely blind in his plan to marry his sister to Antony? Does Antony return to the East for the love of Cleopatra or because his spirit is overpowered when he is near Octavius? 'Although the play continually raises questions about motives, it simply does not give clear answers to them' (Adelman, 15). Leaving aside the question as to whether or not a play should provide 'clear answers', Adelman's formulations have the effect of reducing the political dimensions to the personal; that of Antony's 'spirit' being 'overpowered when he is near Octavius'. That is, of course, what the soothsayer tells him (2. 3. 19–21, 23–8). But why should that explanation be privileged above all others?

For Barbara J. Bono (1984), 'Roman moral absolutism arguably hastens Antony's audience with Cleopatra, hardening inclination into irrevocable choice. Ambivalent, rather than consciously treacherous in his relationship with the two women, and constrained by Caesar's power, Antony is as willing to bend in Cleopatra's direction as Octavius is to cut short Octavia's meditation and define Antony as the enemy. Although the Romans continue to mourn his fall from former greatness, their condemnation is unequivocal'.[2] I presume that by 'moral' here Bono intends 'political'. She points out that the Roman leaders, in 'their drive to make one world' (that is to say, expand and consolidate the Roman empire) seek to isolate Antony's fall from wider implications. Strictly speaking, on the basis of the evidence in the text, it is Octavius who does so. On being told of Antony's death, his first reaction, speaking on behalf of Rome but clearly also on behalf of his own particular role in the tale of this 'pair of chaps', is about the need for respect for formalities:

The breaking of so great a thing should make
A greater crack. The round world
Should have shook lions into civil streets,
And citizens to their dens. The death of Anthony
Is not a single doom, in the name lay
A moeity of the world.

(5. 1. 14–18).

Almost immediately after, however, Octavius not only places the blame upon his adversary; he also suggests that little of what had transpired is his fault – rather that what had happened could be explained by the fact that 'we do lance/ Diseases in our bodies' (5. 1. 3. 36–7).

Alternatively stated, his view is that the Roman body politic under his administration is in excellent condition. It is sometimes threatened by 'disease', but he has the medicine with which to 'lance' and cure it. If the entry of the 'Egyptian' messenger from Cleopatra puts an abrupt end to this indulgence in speculation, it is his reply to the messenger that places his political practice as well as his self-image into focus. Cleopatra, he says, 'soon shall know of us, by some of ours,/ How honourable and how kindly we/ Determine for her. For Caesar cannot live/ To be ungentle' (5. 1. 57–60). It is this speech, with its two untruths that exemplifies the nature of the 'moral absolutism' (Bono) that drives Antony to becoming a 'chronic deserter' (Schanzer) and to show how his 'spirit' is overpowered (Adelman).

But all of those still see these events through Roman eyes. Two recent critics have sought to break out from under that restriction. Making using of Eve Kosofsky Sedgwick's notion of 'homosocial desire' referred to earlier, Coppélia Kahn, asserts that 'Despite the obvious contrasts of character that distinguish Antony and Caesar, they mirror each other in a blinding desire for *imperium* ... Emulation binds them because they are rivals for power'. Such a view is, of course, right. But only to a limited extent. Kahn herself goes on to state that 'The embracing irony of the play is that Antony never returns to the heroic Roman image of fixed and stable identity from which – according to the testimony of nearly every character in the play – he has temporarily departed'.[3]

The effect of having 'temporarily departed' from that 'Roman image of fixed and stable identity' is that, in the words of Linda

70

Charnes (1993), 'Antony comes to realize that he is occupying an untenable position as a kind of "sojourner" in his own life – one who exists between places, unembedded, without the firmness of identity provided by unwavering allegiance to a particular place. The more Antony sojourns emotionally, imaginatively, and literally between Rome and Egypt (and the two subject positions they offer and mutually critique), the more unconstituted his identity becomes. It is this experience of "infirm" boundaries, of being unidentical to himself and what he has been in the past, that becomes intolerable to him...In this position of total insecurity, Antony becomes like the land Roman imperialism seeks to conquer: vulnerable to continual remappings and reappropriations of his own subjective terrain'. Importantly, for Charnes, 'Antony's identity as Roman was never his "own" anyway, being a function of Octavius' larger strategy in the intertextual history that already precedes him. That is to say, Antony's identity as "Antony" belongs properly to the larger body of historiography that is the story of Rome'.[4]

'THE COLONIZER WHO REFUSES'

Most of the arguments cited above were chosen deliberately in order to demonstrate the richness and suggestiveness of the explanations offered in the burgeoning variety of critical theory stemming from feminist theories and from psychoanalysis. But terms such as 'deserter', 'sojourner', 'imperium', 'absolutism' all have equally strong political attachments. And, since the burden of my story has been to seek to locate the text in the political contexts of its gestation as well as subsequent transmigrations – 'It is shaped, sir, like itself, and it is as broad as it hath breadth. It is just so high as it is, and moves with its own organs. It lives by that which nourisheth it, and the elements once out of it, it transmigrates' (2. 7. 41–4) – I would like to offer an explanation that is located in political theory, notably that having to do with colonialism and imperialism. It is to be found in Albert Memmi's now-classic *The Colonizer and the Colonized*.[5] But first, some further examples from the text. Despite Antony's sense of duty towards Rome: that 'These strong Egyptian fetters I must break' and that he 'must from this enchanting queen break off' and

71

that 'the strong necessity of time commands' his 'services awhile', his 'full heart/ Remains in use' with her (1. 2. 116, 128; 1. 3. 43–4) – 'By the fire/That quickens Nilus' slime', he assures her that he leaves as 'Thy soldier-servant, making peace or war/ As thou affects' (1. 3. 68–71). Next, the first message he sends, together with an 'Orient pearl' is that he 'will piece/ Her opulent throne with kingdoms. All the East/...shall call her mistress' (1. 5. 45–7). Finally, he tells Eros that he had 'made these wars for Egypt, and the Queen – / Whose heart I thought I had, for she had mine,/ Which, whilst it was mine, had annexed unto't/ A million more, now lost –' (4. 15. 15–18). His objectives could not have been more clearly stated.

The explanation for such actions are to be found in Memmi, who was born in French colonial Tunisia, interred in a forced-labour camp by the German occupiers of that country, and subsequently participated in the Tunisian nationalist independence struggle, and who now lives in Paris, makes a distinction between the colonizer, motivated by three discoveries – profit; privilege; usurpation[6] – and 'the colonizer who refuses', one who 'can no longer agree to become what his fellow citizens have become' with the consequence that

> from now on he lives his life under the sign of contradiction which looms at every step, depriving him of all coherence, and all tranquillity.
>
> What he is actually renouncing is part of himself, and what he slowly becomes as soon as he accepts life in a colony. He participates in and benefits from those privileges which he half-heartedly denounces...
>
> If he persists, he will learn that he is launching into an undeclared conflict with his own people which will always remain alive, unless he returns to the colonialist fold or is defeated. Wonder has been expressed at the vehemence of colonizers against any among them who put colonization in jeopardy. It is clear that such a colonizer is nothing but a traitor. He challenges their very existence and endangers the very homeland which they represent in the colony.[7]

That, briefly stated, seems to me to be the most satisfactory explanation for the conflicts between the 'sole sir o'the'world' and his antagonist – not a 'deserter', but a colonizer who refuses that role and, instead, sides with the descendant of former colonizers now engaged in the defence – indeed, attempt at extension – of the national interest. He is a familiar figure in our postcolonial times. If Octavius is the example of the familiar ethnocentric essentialist, Antony is that equally familiar figure whose project Memmi (in the process of describing himself, in a recent interview) characterizes as follows: 'All of my work has been in sum an inventory of my attachments; all my work has been, it should be understood, a constant revolt against my attachments; all of my work, for certain, has been an attempt at...reconciliation between the different parts of myself'.[8] That description fits Antony perfectly. That the 'colonizer who refuses' allies himself with the defender of this national interest who does so by means of 'playful disruptions of...gender polarities' to reveal the much-vaunted Roman notions of 'order' and 'stability' as being simply 'a contingent fiction, subject to revision',[9] also – and perhaps above all – makes *Antony and Cleopatra the* text for its time. Even more than (say) *The Tempest*, it stands on the threshold of the moment when England will begin the long process of transforming itself from an island offshore from the continent of Europe and, later, claim to have surpassed Rome as imperial power. But it also speaks to the moment of our present dis-contents. If *The Tempest* is the text that explores the real relations that mar(k) colonial encounter, then *Antony and Cleopatra* is the text that speaks dis-ruption and resistance. Cleopatra may claim that she will 'do't after the high Roman fashion' (4. 16. 88), but she disrupts even that. When she is 'again for Cydnus,/ To meet Mark Anthony' (5. 2. 228–9), she has 'nothing/ Of woman in me – now from head to foot/ I am marble constant' (5. 2. 238–40). She is Isis: Egyptian; beneficent mother goddess; bringer of fertility; guarantor of harvests that will ensure culture, as well as agriculture. And all that, despite 'the lies, alas, unparalleled' that continue to be told about her. It is in all those senses that *Antony and Cleopatra* is a text for our times that is 'past the size of dreaming'.

Appendix A: Chronology

82 BCE	Mark Antony born.
69 BCE	Cleopatra born.
65 BCE	Julius Caesar and Crassus plan to annex Egypt. Attempt fails.
64 BCE	End of Seleucid empire, founded 321 BCE by Seleucus Nicanor, one of Alexander the Great's generals. Ruled most of Asia Minor and Persia. Syria becomes a Roman province.
63 BCE	Octavius born (dies 14 CE).
59 BCE	Ptolemy XI Neos Dionysos ('Auletes') recognized as king by Roman state at instigation of Julius Caesar.
58 BCE	Ptolemy XI forced to flee to Rome – deposed by people of Alexandria for his misrule.
55 BCE	Aulus Gabinius, Roman proconsul in Syria, and Mark Antony (then his cavalry commander) restore Ptolemy to Egyptian throne. While in Rome the Egyptian had made the Roman Senate the executors of his will and Pompey the Great the guardian of his son Ptolemy XII (later to be husband to and co-ruler of Egypt with Cleopatra).
51 BCE	Death of Ptolemy XI. Ptolemy XII and Cleopatra joint rulers.
48 BCE	Cleopatra, having disagreed with her co-ruler's advisers (notably the eunuch Photinus), is driven out of Egypt. Flees to Syria. Battle of Pharsalus; Julius Caesar decisively defeats Pompey the Great. Latter flees to Egypt as place of refuge, but is murdered by/on advice of Photinus (A&C 3. 7. 32).

74

47 BCE	Julius Caesar's Alexandrian war. Ptolemy XII defeated. Later drowns in Nile – probably accidentally. Cleopatra restored to throne. Cleopatra/Julius Caesar liaison. Birth of Ptolemy Caesar, a.k.a. Caesarion (*A&C*, 1. 5. 29–33; 2. 3. 234).
46 BCE	Cleopatra in Rome – probably to 44 BCE.
44 BCE	Julius Caesar assassinated (*JC*, 3. 1. 73); Cleopatra returns to Egypt.
43 BCE	Consuls Hirtius and Pansa killed at Mutina (Modena) (*A&C*, 1. 4. 57ff). Second triumvirate instituted: Octavius, Antony and Lepidus.
42 BCE	Battle of Philippi (*JC*, 5. 1). Cassius, Brutus commit suicide (*JC*, 5. 3. 60; 5. 5. 51).
41 BCE	Fulvia (Antony's third wife) and Lucius Antonius (his brother) make war against each other, then against Octavius: Perusine War (*A&C*, 1. 2. 37–95; 2. 2. 99–103); Cleopatra sails up river Cydnus and meets Antony at Tarsus. Later spends winter of 41–40 in Alexandria. During these months the Parthians invade eastern regions of Roman empire.
40 BCE	Fulvia dies in Sicyon (*A&C*, 1. 2. 117–19). Pact of Brundusium and marriage of Antony and Octavia. Sextus Pompey occupies Sardinia and Corsica. Cleopatra gives birth to twins fathered by Antony.
39 BCE	Agreement of Misenum between Octavius, Antony and Pompey (*A&C*, 2. 6). Antony and Octavia set up home in Athens (*A&C*, 3. 4). Antony's commander Ventidius defeats Parthians.
38 BCE	War between Octavius and Pompey. Ventidius victorious for second time in battle with Parthians. Death of Pacorus (*A&C*, 2. 3. 38–40; 3. 1).

37 BCE	Antony and Octavia separate at Corfu. They agree that she should go to Rome to negotiate on his behalf with her brother (*A&C*, 3. 6. 55–9). Pact of Tarentum an attempt to renew the triumvirate. Rumour – probably unfounded – of marriage between Antony and Cleopatra at Antioch.
36 BCE	Octavius, Lepidus and Taurus pursue war against Pompey. Latter defeated by Octavius off Naulochus (*A&C*, 3. 2. 1). Lepidus stripped of position as one of triumvirs by Octavius (*A&C*, 3. 5. 5–10; 3. 6. 32). Meanwhile, Antony unsuccessful in his campaign against Parthians.
35 BCE	Octavia returns to Athens with troop reinforcements and provisions for Antony. He sends her back to Rome. Pompey is killed in Asia Minor (*A&C*, 3. 6. 14–18).
34 BCE	Alexandria. Antony celebrates military victories in Armenia. The 'Donations' of Alexandria: Cleopatra named 'Queen of Kings'; Caesarion 'King of Kings'; client kingdoms distributed to other children (*A&C*, 3. 6. 1–18).
33 BCE	Rulers of client states take oath of allegiance to Antony as a person rather to Roman state (*A&C*, 3. 6. 66–75). Meanwhile, in Rome, propaganda war against Antony and Cleopatra intensifies.
32 BCE	Antony divorces Octavia. His will published in Rome. Senate declares war – against Cleopatra alone.
31 BCE	Octavius assembles fleet off Brundusium and Tarentum. Battle of Actium (*A&C*, 3. 7; 3. 8; 3. 9; 3.10). Antony and Cleopatra flee to Egypt.
30 BCE	Octavius enters Alexandria (*A&C*, 5. 1). Antony and Cleopatra commit suicide (*A&C*, 4. 16. 64; 5. 2. 311). Egypt incorporated into Roman empire.

Appendix B: Stage Productions

Date	Place	Director	Cleopatra	Antony	Octavius	Lepidus	Octavia	Enobarbus	Pompey
1972	Stratford-upon-Avon	Trevor Nunn	Janet Suzman	Richard Johnson	Corin Redgrave	Raymond Westhill	Mary Rutherford	Patrick Stewart	Tim Piggott-Smith
1977	Prospect from the Old Vic	Toby Robertson	Barbara Jefford	John Turner	Terence Wilton	John Rowe	Daphne Rogers	Kenneth Gilbert	Trevor Martin
1977	Edinburgh International Festival: Prospect Theatre	Toby Robertson	Dorothy Tutin	Alec McCowen	Derek Jacobi	John Nettleton	Bernice Stegers	Timothy West	Rupert Fraser
1978	Stratford-upon-Avon	Peter Brook	Glenda Jackson	Alan Howard	Jonathan Pryce	Paul Brooke	Marjorie Bland	Patrick Stewart	David Suchet
1982	The Other Place, Stratford-upon-Avon	Adrian Noble	Helen Mirren	Michael Gambon	Jonathan Pryce	Paul Webster	Penelope Beaumont	Bob Peck	Cive Wood

Date	Place	Director	Cleopatra	Antony	Octavius	Lepidus	Octavia	Enobarbus	Pompey
1987	National Theatre, London	Peter Hall	Judi Dench	Anthony Hopkins	Tim Piggott-Smith	John Bluthal	Sally Dexter	Michael Bryant	David Schofield
1991	Talawa Theatre Co., Bloomsbury Theatre, London	Yvonne Webster	Dona Croll	Jeffery Kissoon	Ben Thomas	Ilario Bisi-Pedro	Yvette Harris	Renu Setna	David Carr
1995	Moving Theatre Co., Riverside Theatre, London	Vanessa Redgrave	Vanessa Redgrave	Paul Butler	Howard Saddler	Stephen MacDonald	Aicha Natalie Kossoko	David Harewood	Andy MacEwan
1998	Royal National Theatre, London	Sean Mathias	Helen Mirren	Alan Rickman	Samuel West	Raad Rawl	Katia Caballero	Finbar Lynch	Danny Sapani
1998	Hackney Empire, London	Michael Bogdanov	Cathy Tyson	Tim Woodward	David Shelley	David Mara	Clare Maguire	John Labonowski	Clive Arrindell

Notes

CHAPTER 1. INTRODUCTION: 'BEHOLD AND SEE'

1 T. J. B. Spencer (ed.), *Shakespeare's Plutarch* (Harmondsworth: Penguin, 1964), 199.
2 Catherine Belsey, *The Subject of Tragedy: Identity and Difference in Renaissance Drama* (London: Methuen, 1985), 1.

CHAPTER 2. THEORIES: 'ALL LENGTH IS TORTURE'

1 T. J. B. Spencer, *Shakespeare: The Roman Plays*, Writers and Their Work, 157, British Council/National Book League (London: Longmans, Green & Co., 1963), 9.
2 Theodore Meron, *Henry's Wars and Shakespeare's Laws: Perspectives on the Law of War in the Later Middle Ages* (Oxford: Clarendon, 1993), ch. 9, pp. 154–71.
3 Spencer, *Shakespeare*, 29.
4 William Hazlitt, 'Characters of Shakespeare's Plays: *Antony and Cleopatra*', in *Complete Works*, ed. P. P. Howe (London: J. M. Dent, 1930), vol. 4, p. 230.
5 T. M. Raysor (ed.), *Coleridge's Shakespearean Criticism*, rev. ed. (London: J. M. Dent, 1960), vol. 1, p. 77.
6 Bernard Shaw, 'Better than Shakespear?', in *Three Plays for Puritans* (Harmondsworth: Penguin, 1946), 29.
7 G. Wilson Knight, *The Imperial Theme* (London: Methuen, 1931; rev. ed. 1965), 200.
8 Irving Ribner, *Patterns in Shakespearean Tragedy* (London: Methuen, 1960), 168–9.
9 S. L. Bethell, *Shakespeare and the Popular Dramatic Tradition* (London: P. S. King & Staples, 1944), 129.
10 Henri Fluchère, *Shakespeare*, trans. Guy Hamilton, with a Foreword by T. S. Eliot (London: Longmans, Green & Co., 1953), 258, 263.

11 Benedetto Croce, *Ariosto, Shakespeare and Corneille*, trans. Douglas Ainslie (London: Allen & Unwin, 1920), 241–2.

12 Benedetto Croce, *Philosophy – Poetry – History: An Anthology of Essays*, trans. Cecil Sprigge (London: Oxford University Press, 1966), 239.

13 Morris Weitz, 'Literature without Philosophy: *Antony and Cleopatra*', *Shakespeare Survey*, 28 (1975), pp. 29–30, col. 2; p. 31, cols. 1 and 2.

14 L. C. Knights, *Some Shakespearean Themes* (London: Chatto & Windus, 1959), 143ff.

15 Franklin M. Dickey, *Not Wisely But Too Well: Shakespeare's Love Tragedies* (San Marino, CA: Huntingdon Library, 1957).

16 J. Leeds Barroll, 'Antony and Pleasure', *JEGP*, 57 (1958), 708–20; Shakespeare and Roman History', *MLR*, 53 (1958), 327–43.

17 William Hazlitt, 'Characters of Shakespeare's Plays' (1817), in John Russell Brown (ed.), *Antony and Cleopatra: A Casebook* (London: Macmillan, 1968).

18 A. C. Bradley, *Oxford Lectures on Poetry* (1909; London: Macmillan, 1934), 304, 294, 296, 297, 301.

19 George Brandes, *William Shakespeare, a Critical Study* (1898), trans. William Archer and Diana White (New York: F. Unger, 1963), 144.

20 John F. Danby, *Poets on Fortune's Hill: Studies in Sidney, Shakespeare, Beaumont and Fletcher* (London: Faber, 1952), 132.

21 John Drakakis (ed.), *'Antony and Cleopatra': A New Casebook* (London: Macmillan, 1994), 8–9.

22 Terence Eagleton, *Shakespeare and Society* (New York: Schocken, 1967), 123.

23 Terry Eagleton, *William Shakespeare* (Oxford: Basil Blackwell, 1986), 87–88.

24 Linda Fitz, 'Egyptian Queens and Male Reviewers: Sexist Attitudes in *Antony and Cleopatra* Criticism', *Shakespeare Quarterly*, 28/3, 297–316.

25 Rosa E. Grindon, *Shakespeare and his Plays from A Woman's Point of View* (Manchester: The Policy Holder Journal Company, 1930).

26 Fitz cites, among others, Harold C. Goddard, *The Meaning of Shakespeare* (Chicago: University of Chicago Press, 1951), vol. 2, p. 199; S. Bethell, *Shakespeare and the Popular Dramatic Tradition* (London: Staples, 1944), 128; Algernon Charles Swinburne, *A Study of Shakespeare* (1880; London: Chatto & Windus, 1902), 189; E. E. Stoll, *Poets and Playwrights* (Minneapolis: University of Minnesota Press, 1930), 13; Harley Granville-Barker, *Prefaces to Shakespeare* (London: Batsford, 1930), vol. 3, p. 91; and Daniel Stempel who, in his article 'The Transmigration of the Crocodile' *Shakespeare Quarterly*, 7, 1956), bases his whole argument on Renaissance misogynistic writings.

27 To cite a selection which fall into this category: Carolyn Lenz, Ruth

Swift, Gayle Green and Carol Neely, *The Woman's Part: Feminist Criticism of Shakespeare'*, (Urbana: University of Illinois Press, 1980); Jean E. Howard and Marion F. O'Connor, *Shakespeare Reproduced: The Text in History and Ideology* (New York and London: Methuen, 1987); Penny Gay, *Shakespeare's Unruly Women* (London and New York: Routledge, 1994); Dympna Callaghan, Lorraine Helms and Jyotsna Singh, *The Weyward Sisters: Shakespeare and Feminist Politics* (Oxford: Blackwell, 1994).

28 Coppélia Kahn, *Man's Estate: Masculine Identity in Shakespeare* (Berkeley: University of California Press, 1981), 193.

29 Ania Loomba and Martin Orkin (eds.), *Post-Colonial Shakespeares* (London and New York: Routledge), 1998.

30 Peter Erickson, *Rewriting Shakespeare: Rewriting Ourselves* (Berkeley and Los Angeles: University of California Press, 1991).

31 Linda Bamber, *Comic Women, Tragic Men: A study of gender and genre in Shakespeare* (Stanford: Stanford University Press, 1982), 48.

32 Edward Said, *Orientalism: Western Conceptions of the Orient* (London: Penguin, 1987), 2–3.

33 Rana Kabbani, *Europe's Myths of Orient: Devise and Rule* (London: Pandora, 1986), 23.

34 Kenneth Parker (ed.), *Early Modern Tales of Orient: A Critical Anthology* (London: Routledge, 1999).

CHAPTER 3.   ROME: 'TO DRENCH THE CAPITOL'

1 M. W. MacCallum, *Shakespeare's Roman Plays and their Background* (London: Macmillan & Co, 1910, reissued 1967), 01.

2 J. E. Phillips, *The State in Shakespeare's Greek and Roman Plays* (New York: Columbia University Press, 1940; repr. New York: Octagon, 1972); J. A. K. Thompson, *Shakespeare and the Classics* (London: Allen & Unwin, 1952); Reuben A. Brower, *Hero and Saint: Shakespeare and the Graeco-Roman Heroic Tradition* (Oxford: Oxford University Press, 1971); J. L. Simmons, *Shakespeare's Pagan World: The Roman Tragedies* (Charlottesville: University of Ohio Press, 1973); Paul A. Cantor, *Shakespeare's Rome: The Roman Tragedies* (Cambridge: Cambridge University Press, 1976); Robert Miola, *Shakespeare's Rome* (Cambridge: Cambridge University Press, 1983); Vivian Thomas, *Shakespeare's Roman Worlds* (London and New York: Routledge, 1989); Geoffrey Miles, *Shakespeare and the Constant Romans* (Oxford: Clarendon, 1996).

3 G. Wilson Knight, *The Imperial Theme: Further Interpretations of Shakespeare's Tragedies including the Roman Plays* (Oxford: Oxford University Press, 1931).

4   Maurice Charney, *Shakespeare's Roman Plays: The Function of Imagery in the Drama* (Cambridge, MA: Harvard University Press, 1961; Ernest Schanzer, *The Problems Plays of Shakespeare: A study of 'Julius Caesar', 'Measure for Measure', 'Antony and Cleopatra'* (London: Routledge & Kegan Paul, 1963); Janet Adelman, *The Common Liar: An Essay on 'Antony and Cleopatra'* (London and New Haven: Yale University Press, 1973); John Wilders. *The Lost Garden: A View of Shakespeare's English and Roman Histories* (London: Macmillan, 1984).

5   August W. von Schlegel, *A Course of Lectures on Dramatic Art and Literature*, trans. from the German by John Black, 2 vols. (London, 1815; repr. 1840, 1846). Quoted in M. Spevack, *A New Variorum Edition of Shakespeare's 'Antony and Cleopatra'* (New York: Modern Language Association of America, 1991), 625.

6   Hermann Ulrici, *Shakespeare's Dramatic Art* (1839; 2nd ed. 1847; 3rd ed. 1868–9; trans. from 3rd German edn. by Dora L. Schmitz, 2 vols. 1876), quoted in Spevack, 202–3.

7   Phillips, *The State in Shakespeare's Greek and Roman Plays*, quoted in Spevack, *Shakespeare's 'Antony and Cleopatra'*, 627.

8   Geoffrey Bullough, *Narrative and Dramatic Sources in Shakespeare: The Roman Plays*, vol. 5 (London: Routledge & Kegan Paul, 1964), 319.

9   J. Simmons, *Shakespeare's Pagan World*, 13–14.

10 Gary B. Miles, 'How Roman are Shakespeare's "Romans"?', *SQ*, 40:3 (1989), 272.

11 Geoffrey Miles, *Shakespeare and the Constant Romans*, 170, 173.

12 Robert Miola, *Shakespeare's Rome* (Cambridge: Cambridge University Press, 1983), 186.

13 Gary B. Miles, 'How Roman are Shakespeare's "Romans"?', 260.

14 Marjorie Garber, *Shakespeare's Ghost Writers: Literature as Uncanny Causality* (London and New York: Methuen, 1987).

15 David Bevington (ed.), *Antony and Cleopatra* (Cambridge: Cambridge University Press, 1990), 255.

16 Phillips, *The State in Shakespeare's Greek and Roman Plays*, 198–200.

17 Charney, *Shakespeare's Roman Plays*, 91.

18 Harold S. Wilson, *On the Design of Shakespearian Tragedy* (Toronto, 1957), 161; quoted in Charney *Shakespeare's Roman Plays*, 91.

19 J. Leeds Barroll, 'Shakespeare and Roman History', *MLR*, 53 (1958), 327–43.

20 J. Leeds Barroll, *Shakespearean Tragedy: Genre, Tradition and Change in 'Antony and Cleopatra'* (Washington: Folger Shakespeare Library, 1984), 201.

21 Julian Markels, *The Pillar of the World: Antony and Cleopatra in Shakespeare's Development* (Columbus, OH: Ohio State University Press, 1968), 126.

22 William Fulbecke, *An historical collection of the continuall factions . . . of*

the Romans and the Italians...before the peaceable Empire of Augustus Caesar (London: W. Ponsonby, 1601), 17.

23 See Bullough, *Narrative and Dramatic Sources of Shakespeare*, p. 278, for the Plutarch story about Antony taking over Pompey's father's house.

24 For the story of Pompey's murder, see Appian, 1578, p. 369.

25 While virtually all other editions have the word 'chaps', Neill has 'chops', for which usage he argues as follows: 'The metaphor reduces all action in the political world to the grinding of two voracious jaws: the ambitions of Anthony and Caesar have come to resembles the "universal wolf" of self-devouring appetite in *Troilus* (1. 3. 121–4) – no matter how much food is thrown to them, each in the end must consume the other' (*Antony and Cleopatra*, World's Classics, Oxford University Press, 1994, p. 230). I am not convinced. The discussion here is in the context of 'the poor third of the world', Lepidus, being 'up, till death enlarge his confine'.

26 Coppélia Kahn, *Roman Shakespeare: Warriors, Wounds and Women* (London and New York: Routledge, 1997), 112–13. The reference is to E. K. Sedgwick, *Between Men: English Literature and Male Homosexual Desire* (New York: Columbia University Press, 1985), 2.

27 Victor Kiernan, *Eight Tragedies of Shakespeare: A Marxist Study* (London: Verso, 1996), 170–71.

28 Bevington, in his edition of *Antony and Cleopatra*, glosses the phrase as 'three-sectored: Europe, Asia, Africa', henceforward to be governed not by the three triumvirs but by Caesar Augustus. He further cites Donald K. Anderson, Jr., in *ELN*, 17 (1979), pp. 103–6 for ' "nook" to mean "sector of a circle" ', with the image being taken from the so-called Tin-O-maps in which a T, inscribed within a circle, divides that circle into three sectors, with the one representing Asia being twice the size of the other two'. Neill, too, refers to the political division of the world between the triumvirs, or the three continents, but he also mentions other possibilities, notably the so-called racial division among the offspring of the three sons of Noah (Shem; Ham; Japhet) or the elemental division into earth, sea, and sky (Ovid's *triplex mundus*).

29 For the story of Alexas, see Bullough, *Narrative and Dramatic Sources of Shakespeare*, 306.

30 See Appian, p. 373. *An ancient history...of the Roman wars, both civil and foreign* (London: Ralph Newberg and Henry Bynniman, 1578), 373.

31 I am grateful to Allesandro Vescovi for drawing my attention to this translation.

CHAPTER 4. EGYPT: 'A LASS UNPARALLELED'

1 Andrew Borde, *The fyrst boke of the Introduction to knowledge. The whych dothe teache a man to speake parte of all maner of languages, and to know the usage and fashion of all maner of countreys* ... Imprinted at (London: William Copland, 1550).

2 Thomas Harman, *A caveat or warening of commen cursetors* (London: Wylliam Gryffith, 1566; John Cowell, *The Interpreter* (Cambridge: John Legate, 1607); Samuel Rid, *Lanthorne and Candlelight* (London: John Busbie, 1608); A. V. Judges, *The Elizabethan Underworld* (London: George Routledge, 1930; repr., London: Routledge & Kegan Paul, 1965). See also Gamni Salgado, *Coney-Catchers and Bawdy-Baskets: An Anthology of Elizabethan Law Life* (Harmondsworth: Penguin, 1972).

3 A. L. Beier, *Masterless Men: The Vagrancy Problem in England 1560–1640* (London: Methuen, 1985); Christopher Hill, *The World Turned Upside Down: Radical Ideas during the English Revolution* (1972: Harmondsworth: Penguin, 1975), ch. 3.

4 Catherine Belsey, 'Cleopatra's Seduction', in *Alternative Shakespeares 2*, ed. Terence Hawkes (London: Routledge, 1996), 48.

5 David Bevington (ed.), *Antony and Cleopatra* (Cambridge: Cambridge University Press, 1990), p. 91, note to ll. 149–50.

6 Shakespeare here confuses father and son, Cneius Pompeius Magnus (106–48 BCE) and Sextus Pompeius (d. 45 BCE).

7 Neill is the first editor to use 'ribanded'. The more conventional use is 'ribaudred' (the only occurrence of the word in the language). There have been various versions, including 'ribald-rid'. M. R. Ridley (Arden edn., 1954); Bevington (New Cambridge, 1990); Wilders (Arden, 1995) all use 'ribaudred', while Greenblatt (Norton Shakespeare, 1997) uses 'riband-red', which is glossed as 'Decked in ribbons. This emendation ... juxtaposes the image of Cleopatra bedecked like a horse or a whore with the red tokens of the plague'.

8 Linda Bamber, *Comic Women, Tragic Men: A Study of Gender and Genre in Shakespeare* (Stanford, CA: Stanford University Press, 1982.

9 Phyllis Rackin, 'Anti-Historians: Women's Roles in Shakespeare's Histories', *Theatre Journal*, 37 (October 1985), 329.

10 Linda Woodbridge, *Women and the English Renaissance: Literature and the Nature of Womankind, 1540–1620* (Urbana: University of Illinois Press, 1984), 208.

11 August W. von Schlegel, quoted in Marvin Spevack, *A New Variorum Edition of Shakespeare's 'Antony and Cleopatra'* (New York: The Modern Language Association of America, 1991), 416–17.

12 William Hazlitt, *Characters of Shakespeare's Plays: Antony and Cleopatra*, first published as *A View of the English Stage or a Series of Dramatic*

Criticisms, 1813; quoted in Spevack, *Shakespeare's 'Antony and Cleopatra'*, 688.

13 Thomas MacAlindon, *Shakespeare and Decorum* (London: Macmillan, 1973), 209–10.

14 L. L. Shücking, *Character Problems in Shakespeare's Plays*, trans. 1922, (London: Harrap, 1922); quoted in Spevack, *Shakespeare's 'Antony and Cleopatra'*, 694.

15 Leo Kirschbaum, *Character and Characterization in Shakespeare* (Detroit: Wayne State University Press, 1962), 103, 107; quoted from Spevack, *Shakespeare's 'Antony and Cleopatra'*, 696.

16 Algernon Charles Swinburne, *A Study of Shakespeare* (London: Chatto, 1879); G. Wilson Knight, *The Imperial Theme: Further Interpretations of Shakespeare's Tragedies including the Roman Plays* (Oxford: Oxford University Press, 1931; rev. edn., London: Methuen, 1965); quoted in Spevack, *Shakespeare's 'Antony and Cleopatra'*, 696.

17 Kiernan, *Eight Tragedies of Shakespeare*, 161, 163.

18 E. A. J. Honigmann, *Shakespeare. Seven Tragedies: The Dramatist's Manipulation of Response* (London: Macmillan, 1976), 160–62.

19 H. W. Fawkner, *Shakespeare's Hyperontology: 'Antony and Cleopatra'* (Rutherford/Madison/Teaneck: Farleigh Dickenson University Press, 1990), 84–5, 137.

20 Because of the manner in which a speech, apparently taken down by her chaplain to be read later to the troops who were too far away to hear, and which was not printed until 1651, was subsequently transmitted, the text exists in several versions. There is, however, an interesting corroborative account: *The copie of a letter sent out of England to Don Bernadin Mendoza, Ambassadour in France for the King of Spaine . . . found in the Chamber of Richard Leigh, a Seminarie Priest, who was later executed for High Treason, committed at the time that the Spanish Armada was in the seas* (London, 1580; repr. in *The Harleian Miscellany*, ed. William Oldys and Thomas Park, vol. 1, 1808), p. 152. The fullest and most accessible account of the speech is in Alison Plowden, *Elizabeth Regina: The Age of Triumph, 1558–1603* (New York: Times Books, 1980).

21 T. J. B. Spencer (ed.), *Shakespeare's Plutarch* (Harmondsworth: Penguin, 1964), 206–7.

22 'Now it had been a speech of old time that the family of the Antonii were descended from one Anton, the son of Hercules, whereof the family took name. This opinion did Antonius seek to confirm in all his doings, not only resembling him in the likeness of his body, as we have said before, but also in the wearing of his garments. For when he would openly show himself abroad before many people, he would always wear his cassock girt down low upon his hips,

85

with a great sword dangling by his side, and upon that some ill-favoured cloak' (T. J. B. Spencer, *Shakespeare's Plutarch*, 177).

23 H. B. Lathrop, *Translations from the Classics in English from Caxton to Chapman, 1477–1620* (Madison: University of Wisconsin Press, 1933), 139.

24 Lucy Hughes-Hallett, *Cleopatra: Histories, Dreams, and Distortions* (London: Vintage, 1991), p. 76. See also Madelon Gohlke, ' "I wooed thee with my sword": Shakespeare's Tragic Paradigms', in *Representing Shakespeare: New Psychoanalytic Essays*, ed. Murray M. Schwartz and Coppélia Kahn (Baltimore: Johns Hopkins, 1980).

25 Anne Barton, ' "Nature's Piece 'gainst Fancy": The Divided Catastrophe in *Antony and Cleopatra*', an inaugural lecture, Bedford College, University of London, 1972.

26 John Drakakis, 'Cleopatra's Carnival and the Politics of Comedy', paper presented at the International Shakespeare conference at Stratford-upon-Avon, August 1995. I am indebted to the author for allowing me access to the draft.

27 Janet Adelman, *The Common Liar: An Essay on 'Antony and Cleopatra'* (New Haven and London: Yale University Press, 1973), 184.

28 Ania Loomba, *Gender, Race, Renaissance Drama* (Manchester: Manchester University Press, 1989), 78.

29 Kim F. Hall, *Things of Darkness: Economies of Race and Gender in Early Modern England* (Ithaca and London: Cornell University Press, 1995), 153–4.

30 Joyce Green MacDonald, 'Sex, Race, and Empire in Shakespeare's *Antony and Cleopatra*', *Literature and History*, 5:1 (1996), 60–77.

31 Ania Loomba, 'Shakespeare and Cultural Difference', in *Alternative Shakespeares 2*, ed. Terence Hawkes (London: Routledge, 1996), 164–91.

32 It is worth quoting Aemilia Lanyer in context. Her remarks appear in a section of the poem which, in a side-note, informs that the remarks are addressed 'To my Lady Cumberland'.

> Great Cleopatra's love to Anthony
> Can no way be compared to thine;
> She left her love in his extremity,
> When greatest need should cause her to combine
> Her force with his, to get the victory.
> Her love was earthly, and thy love divine.
> > Her love was only to support her pride
> > Humility thy love doth guide.
>
> That glorious part of Death, which last she played
> To appease the ghost of her deceased love,
> Had never needed, if she could have stayed

When his extremes made trial and did prove
Her leaden love unconstant and afraid.
Their wicked wars the wrath of God might move
    To take revenge for chaste Octavia's wrongs
    Because she enjoys what unto her belongs.
No Cleopatra, though thou were as fair
As any creature in Antonius's eyes
Yea wert thou as rich, as wise, as rare
As any pen could write or wit devise
Yet with this Lady canst thou not compare
Whose inward virtues all thy worth denies.
    Yet though, a black Egyptian dos't appear
    Though false, she's true; and to her love more dear.

She sacrificed to her dearest love
With flowers of faith, and garlands of good deeds.
She flies not from him when afflictions prove;
She bears his cross, and stops his wounds that bleed.
She loves, and lives chaste as the turtledove
She attends upon him, and his flocks she feeds
    Yet for one touch of death which they didst try
A thousand deaths she every day doth die.

Her virtuous life exceeds thy worthy death
Yea, she hath richer ornaments of State
Shining more glorious than in dying breath
Thou didst; when either pride or cruel fate
Did work thee to prevent a double death
To stay the malice, scorn, and cruel hate
    Of Rome, that joy'd to see thy pride pulled down
    Whose beauty wrought to hazard of her crown.

                                  (fr3–v)

33 For instance, the much-translated Latin poet Lucan (Marcus
Annaeus Lucanus; born Cordoba, Spain in 39 CE, a nephew of
Seneca who brought him to Rome at an early age, but who was later
forced to commit suicide by the Emperor Nero at age 26 in 65 CE),
in his story of the civil war between Julius Caesar and Pompey,
commonly known as the *Pharsalia*, had no doubt that the Egyptian
queen had a white skin – one that she was keen to display to her
admirers. The 1614 translation of *Lucan's Pharsalia. Containing the
civill warres betweene Caesar and Pompey. Written in Latine heroicall verse
by M. Annaeus Lucanus. Translated into English verse by Sir Arthur
Gorges, Knight. Whereunto is annexed the life of the authour, collected out
of divers authors.* London. Printed for Edward Blount, 1614 asserts
that

Her rising breasts, that snow white beene
Through the Sydonian lawnes are seene.
Whilst it a vaile doth overshade,
That with the Nylan neede was made
Most curiously with threds compact.
Yet with the combe so nycely slackt,
As that some places being thinne,
It did bewray her lily skinne.

(425–6)

while 1631 translation of the same text, by Thomas May, has the
following: 'Her snowy breasts their whitenesse did display/
Through the thin Sidonian tiffenay' [a kind of transparent silk or
gauze cloth].

34 Martin Bernal, *Black Athena: The Afroasiatic Roots of Classical Civilization* (London: Vintage, vol. 1, 1987; vol. 2. 1991).

35 Mary Lefkowitz, *Not Out of Africa: How Afrocentrism Became an Excuse to Teach Myth as History* (New York: Basic, 1996), esp. pp. 34–52; Frank M. Snowden, Jr., 'Bernal's "Blacks" and the Afrocentrists', in *Black Athena Revisited*, ed. Mary Lefkowitz and Guy MacLean Rogers (Chapel Hill: University of North Carolina Press, 1996), 112–28; V. Y. Mudimbe, 'African Athena?', *Transition*, 58 (1992), 114–23; Mary Hamer, 'Queen of Denial', *Transition*, 72 (1996), 80–93; Molefi Kete Asante, *'Black Athena Revisited'*, *Research in African Literature*, 29:1 (Spring, 1998), 206–10.

36 Jerry Brotton, *Trading Territories: Mapping the Early Modern World* (London: Reaktion Books, 1997).

37 Douglas Chambers, *The Reinvention of the World: English Writing 1650–1750* (London: Arnold, 1996).

38 Kwame Anthony Appiah, *In My Father's House: Africa in the Philosophy of Culture* (New York: Oxford University Press, 1992), esp. ch. 1, 'The invention of Africa', ch. 2, 'Illusions of race', ch. 3, 'Topologies of Nativism', ch. 4, 'The Myth of an African World'; V. Y. Mudimbe, *The Invention of Africa: Gnosis, Philosophy, and the Order of Knowledge* (London: James Currey, 1988).

39 Michael Grant, *Cleopatra* (London: Weidenfeld & Nicolson, 1972); *From Alexander to Cleopatra: The Hellenistic World* (London: Weidenfeld & Nicolson, 1982); Hans Volkmann, *Cleopatra: A Study in Politics and Propaganda* (London: Elek, 1953); Lucy Hughes-Hallett, *Cleopatra: Histories, Dreams and Distortions* (London: Vintage, 1991); Mary Hamer, *Signs of Cleopatra: History, Politics, Representation* (London and New York: Routledge, 1993).

40 I should here, perhaps, add a personal note. I am black, and was born in South Africa; from which country I made a clandestine

departure at the end of 1964 via the then Bechuanaland
Protectorate (now Botswana) and eventually to the United Kingdom where I was (like many others at that time, and from that same
place) given political asylum.

CHAPTER 5. CONCLUSION: 'PAST THE SIZE OF DREAMING'

1 Ernest Schanzer, *The Problem Plays of Shakespeare: A Study of 'Julius
Caesar', 'Measure for Measure', 'Antony and Cleopatra'* (London:
Routledge & Kegan Paul, 1963), 145.
2 Barbara J. Bono, *Literary Transvaluation: From Vergilian Epic to
Shakespearean Tragicomedy* (Berkeley and Los Angeles: University of
California Press, 1984), 162.
3 Coppélia Kahn, *Roman Shakespeare: Warriors, Wounds, and Women*
(London and New York: Routledge, 1997), 113.
4 Linda Charnes, *Notorious Identity: Materializing the Subject* (Cambridge, MA: Harvard University Press, 1993), 113, 115.
5 Albert Memmi, *The Colonizer and the Colonized* (1957), trans. Howard
Greenfield, with a Foreword by Jean-Paul Sartre, and new
introduction by Liam O'Dowd (London: Earthscan, 1990).
6 Memmi, *The Colonizer and the Colonized*, 75.
7 Memmi, *The Colonizer and the Colonized*, 85–7.
8 'Irreconcilable Differences: A Conversation with Albert Memmi',
Transition, 71, New Series, 6:3 (1996), 158.
9 Jyotsna Singh, 'Renaissance Antitheatricality, Antifeminism, and
Shakespeare's *Antony and Cleopatra*', *Renaissance Drama*, 20 (1989),
109, 117.

Select Bibliography

EDITIONS

Andrews, John F., (ed.), *William Shakespeare: Antony and Cleopatra*, Everyman Library (London: J. M. Dent, 1989).

Bevington, David (ed.), *Antony and Cleopatra*, New Cambridge Shakespeare (Cambridge: Cambridge University Press, 1990).

Neill, Michael, (ed.), *Antony and Cleopatra*, World's Classics (Oxford: Oxford University Press, 1994).

Wilders, John, (ed.), *Antony and Cleopatra*, Arden Shakespeare (Routledge, 1995).

CONTEMPORARY TEXTS

Appian, *An ancient history and exquisite chronicle of the Roman wars, both civil and foreign. Written in Greek by the noble orator and historiographer Appian of Alexandria, one of the most learned counsel of the most mighty emperors Trajan and Hadrian. In the which is declared their most greedy desire to conquer others; their moral malice to destroy themselves; their seeking of matters to make war abroad; their picking of quarrels to fall out at home; all the degrees of sedition, and all the effects of ambition; a firm determination of Fate through all the changes of Fortune; and, finally, an evident demonstration that peoples rule must give place and princes power prevail. With a continuation (because that part of Appian is not extant) from the death of Sextus Pompeius, second son to Pompey the Great, till the overthrow of Antony and Cleopatra, after which time Octavius Caesar had the lordship of all alone* (London: Ralph Newbery and Henry Bynniman, 1578).

Bateman, Stephen, *Batman vppon Bartholome, his booke De Proprietatibus Rerum, newly corrected, enlarged and amended: with such additions as are requisite vnto every seuerall booke. Taken foorth of the most approued authors, the like heretofore not translated into English. Profitable for all*

Estates, as well for the benefite of the mind as the bodie (London: Thomas East, 1582).

Boemus, Johannes, *The Fardle of Facions: Conteyning the aunciente maners, customes, and lawes of the people inhabiting the two parts of the earth, Africke and Asie* (1555).

Borde, Andrew, *The fyrst boke of the Introduction to knowledge. The whych dothe teache a man to speake parte of all maner of languages, and to know the usage and fashion of all maner of countreys* (London: William Copland, 1550).

Cope, Anthony, *The historie of the two noble capitaines of the worlde, Anniball and Scipio, translated . . . out of Titus Livius and other authores* (London: Bertheli, 1544).

Cowell, John, *The Interpreter: or Booke conteyning the signification of wordes; wherein is set foorth the true meaning of all or the most of such wordes and terms, as are mentioned in the law writers or statutes of this victorious and renowned kingdome, requiring any exposition or interpretation. A worke not onely profitable, but also necessary for such as desire thoroughly to be instructed in the knowledge of our lawes, statutes, and other antiquities* (Cambridge: Printed by John Legate, 1607).

Crakanthorpe, Richard, *A sermon at the solemnizing of the happie inauguration of our most gracious and religious soueraigne King Iames. Wherein is manifestly proued that the soueraingnty of kings is immediutely from God, and second to no authority on earth whatsoeuer. Preached at Paules Crosse the 14 of March 1608.* (London: W. Iaggard for Tho. Adam, 1609).

Eutropius, *A briefe chronicle, wherein are described shortly the origin and successive estate of the Roman public weal, the alteration and change of sundry offices in the same; the order and succession of the kings, consuls and emperors thereof . . . from the first foundation of the City of Rom. . . . Collected first by Eutropius, and Englished by Nicholas Haward* (1564).

Fulbecke, William, *An historical collection of the continuall factions, tumults, and massacres of the Romans and the Italians, during the space of one hundred and twentie yeares before the peaceable Empire of Augustus Caesar. Selected and derived out of the best writers and reporters of those accidents . . . beginning where the historie of T. Livius doth end, and ending where C. Tacitus doth begin.* (London: W. Ponsonby, 1601; abridged edn. T. E. for R. More, 1608).

Harman, Thomas, *A caveat or warening of commen cursitors, vulgarely called vagabones, set forth by Thomas Harman, Esquire, for the utilitie and proffyt of his natural countrey* (London: William Gryffith, 1566).

Herodian, *The history of Herodian, a Greek author, treating of the Roman emperors after Marcus. Translated out of Greek into Latin by Angelus Politanius, and out of Latin into Englishe by Nicholas Smyth* (London: William Copland, 1550).

Herodotus, *The famous history of Herodotus. Containing the discourse of divers countries; the succession of their kings; the acts and exploits achieved by them; the laws and customs of every nation, with the description of the antiquity of the same. Devided into nine books, entitled with the names of the nine Muses* (London: Thomas Marshe, 1584).

Hubbocke, William, *An oration gratulatory to the high and mighty James of England, Scotland, France and Ireland, king, defender of the faith, &c. On the twelfth day of February last presented, when His Majesty entered the Tower of London to perform the residue of the solemnities of his coronation through the city of London deferred by reason of the plague and published by His Higness's special allowance: wherein both the description of the Tower of London and the union of the kingdomes is compendiously touched* (Oxford: Simon Waterson, 1604).

Josephus, Flavius, *The famous and memorable works of [Flavius] Josephus, a man of much honour and learning among the Jews. Faithfully translated out of the Latin and French by Thomas Lodge* (G. Bishop, S. Waterson, P. Short and Tho. Adams, 1602).

Livy, *The Roman History. Written by T. Livius of Padua . . . with a chronology to the whole history, and a topography of Rome in old time*, transl. out of the Latin into English by Philemon Holland (London: Adam Islip, 1600).

Lucanus, Marcus Annaeus (Lucan), *Pharsalia*, trans. by Sir Arthur Gorges (London: Printed for Edward Blount, 1614).

Phillips, John, *A New History of Ethiopia. Being a full and accurate description of the kingdom of Abessinia. Vulgarly, though erroneously called the Empire of Prester John . . . By the learned Job Ludolphus, Counsellor to His Imperial Majesty and the Dukes of Saxony, and Treasurer to His Highness the Elector Palatine. The second edition. To which is added a new and exact map of the country. And also, a Preface, shewing the usefulness of this history . . . and the author's opinion of some other writers concerning Ethiopia* (London: Samuel Smith, 1684).

Rid, Samuel, *Lanthorne and Candle-light, or the Bell-man's night walk. In which hee brings light to a broode of more strange villainies, than euer were till this yeare discouered* (London: John Busbie, 1608).

Tranquillus, C. Suetonius, *The History of Twelve Caesars, Emperors of Rome. Written in Latin by C. Suetonius Tranquillus, and newly translated into English by Philemon Holland, Doctor of Physick . . .* (London: Matthew Lownes, 1606).

CRITICISM

Adelman, Janet, *The Common Liar: An Essay on 'Antony and Cleopatra'* (New Haven and London: Yale University Press, 1973).

—— *Suffocating Mothers: Fantasies of Maternal Origin in Shakespeare's Plays, 'Hamlet' to 'The Tempest'* (London and New York: Routledge, 1992).

Alvis, John, 'Unity of Subject in Shakespeare's Roman Plays', *Publications of the Arkansas Philological Association*, 3:3 (1977).

—— 'The Religion of Eros: A re-interpretation of *Antony and Cleopatra*', *Renascence*, 30 (1978), 185–98.

Appiah, Kwame Anthony, *In My Father's House: Africa in the Philosophy of Culture* (New York: Oxford University Press, 1992).

Axton, Marie, *The Queen's Two Bodies: Drama and the Elizabethan Succession* (London: Royal Historical Society, 1977).

Baker, Deborah, and Ivo Kamps (eds.), *Shakespeare and Gender: A History* (London and New York, Verso, 1995).

Bamber, Linda, *Comic Women, Tragic Men: A Study of Gender and Genre in Shakespeare* (Stanford: Stanford University Press, 1982).

Barroll, J. Leeds, 'Antony and Pleasure', *JEGP*, 57 (1958), 708–20.

—— 'Shakespeare and Roman History', *MLR*, 53 (1958), 327–43.

—— 'Shakespearean Tragedy: Genre, Tradition, and Change in *Antony and Cleopatra*' (Washington: Folger Shakespeare Library, 1984).

—— *Politics, Plague and Shakespeare's Theater: The Stuart Years* (Ithaca and London: Cornell University Press, 1991).

Barton, Anne, '"Nature's Piece 'gainst Fancy": The Divided Catastrophe in *Antony and Cleopatra*', an inaugural lecture, Bedford College, University of London, 1972.

Bate, Jonathan (ed.), *The Romantics on Shakespeare* (London: Penguin, 1992).

Beier, A. L., *Masterless Men: The Vagrancy Problem in England 1500–1640* (London: Methuen, 1985).

Belsey, Catherine, *The Subject of Tragedy: Identity and Difference in Renaissance Drama* (London: Methuen, 1985).

—— 'Afterword: A Future for Materialist Feminist Criticism?', in *The Matter of Difference: Materialist Feminist Criticism of Shakespeare*, ed. Valerie Wayne (Ithaca: Cornell University Press, 1991).

—— 'Cleopatra's Seduction', in *Alternative Shakespeares* 2, ed. Terence Hawkes (London: Routledge, 1996), 38–62.

Bernal, Martin, *Black Athena: The Afroasiastic Roots of Classical Civilization* (London: Vintage, vol. 1, 1987; vol. 2, 1991).

Bethell, S., L., *Shakespeare and the Popular Dramatic Tradition* (London: P. S. King & Staples, 1944).

Bevington, David, *Tudor Drama and Politics: A Critical Approach to Topical Meaning* (Cambridge, MA: Harvard University Press, 1968).

Bono, Barbara, J., *Literary Transvaluation: From Vergilian Epic to Shakespearean Tragicomedy* (Berkeley and Los Angeles: University of California Press, 1984).

Bradley, A. C., *Oxford Lectures on Poetry* (London: Macmillan, 1909, 1934).

Brandes, George, *William Shakespeare: A Critical Study* (first published 1898), trans. William Archer and Diana White (New York: F. Unger, 1963).

Brotton, Jerry, *Trading Territories: Mapping the Early Modern World* (London: Reaktion Books, 1997).

—— '"This Tunis, sir, was Carthage": Contesting Colonisation in The Tempest', in *Post-Colonial Shakespeares*, ed. Ania Loomba and Martin Orkin (London: Routledge, 1998), 23–42.

Brower, Reuben, A., *Hero and Saint: Shakespeare and the Graeco-Roman Tradition* (Oxford: Oxford University Press, 1971).

Brown, John Russell, (ed)., *Antony and Cleopatra, a Casebook* (London: Macmillan, 1968).

Bullough, Geoffrey, *Narrative and Dramatic Sources of Shakespeare: The Roman Plays*, vol. 5 (London: Routledge & Kegan Paul, 1964).

Bushman, Mary Ann, 'Representing Cleopatra', in *In Another Country: Feminist Perspectives on Renaissance Drama*, ed. Dorothea Kehler and Susan Baker (Metuchen, NY and London: Scarecrow Press, 1991).

Callaghan, Dympna, *Women and Gender in Renaissance Tragedy: A Study of 'King Lear', 'The Duchess of Malfi', and 'The White Devil'* (London: Harvester, 1989).

Callaghan, Dympna, Lorraine Helms and Jyotsna Singh, *The Weyward Sisters: Shakespeare and Feminist Politics* (Oxford: Blackwell, 1984).

Cantor, Paul, A., *Shakespeare's Rome: Republic and Empire* (Ithaca and London: Cornell University Press, 1976).

—— *Shakespeare's Rome: The Roman Tragedies* (Cambridge: Cambridge University Press, 1983).

Chambers, Douglas, *The Reinvention of the World: English Writing 1650–1750* (London: Arnold, 1996).

Charnes, Linda, *Notorious Identity: Materializing the Subject* (Cambridge, MA: Harvard University Press, 1993).

Charney, Maurice, *Shakespeare's Roman Plays: The Function of Imagery in the Drama* (Cambridge, MA: Harvard University Press, 1961).

Croce, Benedetto, *Ariosto, Shakespeare and Corneille*, trans. Douglas Ainslie (London: George Allen & Unwin, 1921).

—— *Philosophy – Poetry – History: An Anthology of Essays*, trans. Cecil Sprigge (London: Oxford University Press, 1966).

Danby, John, F., *Poets on Fortune's Hill: Studies in Sidney, Shakespeare, Beaumont and Fletcher* (London: Faber, 1952).

Dickey, Franklin, M., *Not Wisely But Too Well: Shakespeare's Love Tragedies* (San Marino CA: Huntingdon Library, 1957).

Dollimore, Jonathan, *Radical Tragedy: Religion, Ideology and Power in the Drama of Shakespeare and his Contemporaries* (Brighton: Harvester, 1984).

—— Alan Sinfield (eds.), *Political Shakespeare: New Essays in Cultural*

94

Materialism (Manchester: Manchester University Press, 1985, 2nd edn. 1994).

Drakakis, John, (ed)., *Alternative Shakespeares* (London: Methuen, 1985).

—— *'Antony and Cleopatra': A New Casebook* (Basingstoke: Macmillan, 1994).

Eagleton, Terence, *Shakespeare and Society* (New York: Schocken, 1967).

—— *William Shakespeare* (Oxford: Basil Blackwell, 1986).

Erickson, Peter, *Rewriting Shakespeare, Rewriting Ourselves* (Berkeley and Los Angeles: University of California Press, 1991).

Fawkner, H. W., *Shakespeare's Hyperontology: 'Antony and Cleopatra'*, (Rutherford/Madison/Teaneck: Farleigh Dickenson University Press, 1990).

Fichter, Andrew, *'Antony and Cleopatra: "the Time of Universal Peace"'*, *Shakespeare Survey*, 33 (1980), 99–111.

Fitz, Linda, 'Egyptian Queens and Male Reviewers: Sexist Attitudes in *Antony and Cleopatra* Criticism', *Shakespeare Quarterly*, 28:3 (1977), 297–316.

Fluchère, Henri, *Shakespeare*, trans. Guy Hamilton, with a Foreword by T. S. Eliot (London: Longmans, Green & Co., 1953).

Garber, Marjorie, *Shakespeare's Ghost Writers: Literature as Uncanny Causality* (London and New York: Methuen, 1987).

Gay, Penny, *As She Likes It: Shakespeare's Unruly Women* (London: Routledge, 1994).

Goddard, Harold C., *The Meaning of Shakespeare* (Chicago: University of Chicago Press, 1951).

Gohlke, Madelon, '"I wooed thee with my sword": Shakespeare's Tragic Paradigms', in *Representing Shakespeare: New Psychoanalytic Essays*, ed. Murray M. Schwarz and Coppélia Kahn (Baltimore: Johns Hopkins, 1980).

Grant, Michael, *Cleopatra* (London: Weidenfeld & Nicolson, 1972).

—— *From Alexander to Cleopatra: The Hellenistic World* (London: Weidenfeld & Nicolson, 1982).

Granville-Barker, Harley, *Prefaces to Shakespeare* (London: Batsford, 1930).

Grindon, Rosa, E., *Shakespeare and His Plays from a Woman's Point of View* (Manchester: The Policy Holder Journal Company, 1930).

Hall, Kim, F., *Things of Darkness: Economies of Race and Gender in Early Modern England* (Ithaca and London: Cornwell University Press, 1995).

Hamer, Mary, *Signs of Cleopatra: History, Politics, Representation* (London and New York: Routledge, 1993).

Hawkes, Terence (ed.), *Alternative Shakespeares 2* (London: Routledge, 1996).

Hazlitt, William, 'Characters of Shakespeare's Plays', in *Complete Works*, ed. P. P. Howe, vol. 4 (London: J. M. Dent and Sons, 1930).

Heine, Heinrich, 'Heine on Shakespeare', from 'Notes on Shakespeare's Heroines' (1895), in *The Romantics on Shakespeare*, ed. Jonathan Bate (London: Penguin, 1992.

Heisch, Alison, 'Queen Elizabeth I and the Persistence of Patriarchy', *Feminist Review* 4, (1980), 45–56.

Hendricks, Margo, and Patricia Parker (eds.), *Women, 'Race' and Writing in the Early Modern Period* (London and New York: Routledge, 1994).

Honigmann, E. A. J., *Shakespeare, Seven Tragedies: The Dramatist's Manipulation of Response* (London: Macmillan, 1976).

Howard, Jean E., *Shakespeare's Art of Orchestration: Stage Technique and Audience Response* (Urbana and Chicago: University of Illinois Press, 1984).

—— 'Crossdressing, the Theatre, and Gender Struggle in Early Modern England', *Shakespeare Quarterly*, 39:4 (1988), 418–40.

Howard, Jean E., and Marion F. O'Conor, *Shakespeare Reproduced: The Text in History and Ideology* (London: Methuen, 1987).

Hughes-Hallett, Lucy, *Cleopatra: Histories, Dreams and Distortions* (London: Vintage, 1991).

Hurstfield, Joel, 'The Historical and Social Background', in *A New Companion to Shakespeare Studies*, ed. Kenneth Muir and S. Schoenbaum (Cambridge: Cambridge University Press, 1971), 168–79.

Jardine, Lisa, *Still Harping on Daughters: Women and Drama in the Age of Shakespeare* (Brighton: Harvester, 1983).

—— *Reading Shakespeare Historically* (London and New York: Routledge, 1996).

—— and Anthony Grafton, '"Studied for Action": How Gabriel Harvey Read his Livy', *Past and Present*, 129 (1990), 30–78.

Judges, A. V., (ed.), *The Elizabethan Underworld: A collection of Tudor and Early Stuart tracts and ballads telling of the lives and misdoings of vagabonds, thieves, rogue, and cozeners, and giving some account of the operation of the civil law* (London: George Routledge, 1930).

Kabbani, Rana, *Europe's Myths of Orient: Devise and Rule* (London: Pandora, 1986).

Kahn, Coppélia, *Man's Estate: Masculine Identity in Shakespeare* (Berkeley: University of California Press, 1981).

—— *Roman Shakespeare: Warriors, Wounds and Women* (London and New York: Routledge, 1997).

Kamps, Ivo, ed.), *Materialist Shakespeare* (London and New York: Verso, 1995).

Kiernan, Victor, *Eight Tragedies of Shakespeare: A Marxist Study* (London: Verso, 1996).

Kirschbaum, Leo, *Character and Characterization in Shakespeare* (Detroit: Wayne State University Press, 1962).

Knight, G. Wilson, *The Imperial Theme: Further Interpretations of Shakespeare's Tragedies including the Roman Plays* (Oxford: Oxford University Press, 1931; rev. edn. London: Methuen, 1965).

Knights, L. C., *Some Shakespearean Themes* (London: Chatto & Windus, 1959).

Lathrop, H. B., *Translations from the Classics into English from Caxton to Chapman, 1477–1620* (Madison: University of Wisconsin Press, 1933).

Lefkowitz, Mary, *Not Out of Africa: How Afrocentrism Became an Excuse to Teach Myth as History* (New York: Basic, 1996), esp. pp. 34–52.

Lenz, Carolyn, Ruth Swift, Gayle Green, Carol Neely, *The Woman's Part: Feminist criticism of Shakespeare* (Urbana: University of Illinois Press, 1980).

Loomba, Ania, *Gender, Race, Renaissance Drama* (Manchester: Manchester University Press, 1989).

—— 'Shakespeare and Cultural Difference', in *Alternative Shakespeares 2*, ed. Terence Hawkes (London: Routledge, 1996), 164–91.

—— and Martin Orkin (eds.), *Post-Colonial Shakespeares* (London: Routledge, 1998).

Lucan, *Lucan's Pharsalia. Containing the civill warres betweene Caesar and Pompey. Written in Latine heroicall verse by Annaeus Lucanus. Translated into English vverse by Sir Arthur Georges, knight. Whereunto is annexed the life of the author, collected out of divers authors. London. Printed for Edward Blount*, 1614.

MacAlindon, Thomas, *Shakespeare and Decorum* (London: Macmillan, 1973).

McCallum, M. W., *Shakespeare's Roman Plays and their Background* (London: Macmillan, 1910, 1967).

MacDonald, Joyce Green, 'Sex, Race, and Empire in Shakespeare's *Antony and Cleopatra*', *Literature and History*, 5:1 (1996), 60–77.

MacLachlan, Alistair, *The Rise and Fall of Revolutionary England: An Essay on the Fabrication of Seventeenth-Century History* (London: Macmillan, 1996).

Markels, Julian, *The Pillar of the World: Antony and Cleopatra in Shakespeare's Development* (Columbus, OH: Ohio State University Press, 1968).

Memmi, Albert, *The Colonizer and the Colonized* (1957), trans. by Howard Greenfield, with a Foreword by Jean-Paul Sartre, and a new introduction by Liam O'Dowd (London: Earthscan, 1990).

—— 'Irreconcilable Differences: A Conversation with Albert Memmi', *Transition*, 71, New Series, 6:3 (1996), 158–77.

Meron, Theodore, *Henry's Wars and Shakespeare's Law: Perspectives on the Law of War in the Middle Ages* (Oxford: Clarendon, 1993), ch. 9, pp. 154–71.

Miles, Gary B., 'How Roman are Shakespeare's "Romans"', *SQ*, 40:3 (1989), 257–83.

Miles, Geoffrey, *Shakespeare and the Constant Romans* (Oxford, Clarendon, 1996).

Miola, Robert, *Shakespeare's Rome* (Cambridge: Cambridge University Press, 1983).

Mudimbe, V. Y., *The Invention of Africa: Gnosis, Philosophy, and the Order of Knowledge* (London: James Currey, 1988).

Muir, Kenneth, *The Sources of Shakespeare's Plays* (London: Methuen, 1977).

Mullaney, Steven, *The Place of the Stage: License, Play, and Power in Renaissance England* (Chicago: Chicago University Press, 1988).

Neely, Carol Thomas, *Broken Nuptials in Shakespeare's Plays* (New Haven and London: Yale University Press, 1985).

Parker, Kenneth, (ed.), *Early Modern Tales of Orient: a critical anthology* (London: Routledge, 1999).

Rackin, Phyllis, 'Shakespeare's Boy Cleopatra, the Decorum of Nature, and the Golden World of Poetry, *PMLA*, 87 (1972), 201–12.

———— 'Anti-Historians: Women's Roles in Shakespeare's Histories', *Theatre Journal*, 37 (October 1985), 329–44.

Raysor, T. M. (ed.), *Coleridge's Shakespearean Criticism*, rev. edn., 2 vols (London: J. M. Dent, 1960).

Ribner, Irving, *Patterns of Shakespearean Tragedy* (London: Methuen, 1960).

Russell, Conrad, *The Causes of the English Civil War* (Oxford: Clarendon, 1990).

———— *The Fall of British Monarchies, 1637–1642* (Oxford: Clarendon, 1991).

———— *Unrevolutionary England, 1603–42* (London: Hambledon Press, 1990).

Said, Edward, *Orientalism: Western Conceptions of the Orient* (1978; repr. with a new Afterword, London: Penguin, 1995).

———— 'Orientalism Reconsidered', in *Europe and its Others*, ed. Francis Barker et al. (Colchester: University of Essex, vol. 1, 1985), 14–27.

Schanzer, Ernest, *The Problem Plays of Shakespeare: A Study of 'Julius Caesar', 'Measure for Measure', 'Antony and Cleopatra'* (London: Routledge & Kegan Paul, 1963).

Schlegel, August W. von, *A Course of Lectures on Dramatic Art and Literature*, trans. from the German by John Black, 2 vols. (London, 1815; repr. 1840, 1846).

Sedgwick, Eve Kosofsky, *Between Men: English Literature and Male Homosexual Desire* (New York: Columbia University Press, 1985).

Shaw, Bernard, 'Better than Shakespear?', in *Three Plays for Puritans* (Harmondsworth: Penguin, 1946).

Simmons, J. L., *Shakespeare's Pagan World: The Roman Tragedies* (Charlottesville: University of Ohio Press, 1973).

Singh, Jyotsna, 'Renaissance Antitheatricality, Antifeminism, and Shakespeare's *Antony and Cleopatra*', *Renaissance Drama*, 20 (1989), 99–101.

Snowden, Frank, M., Jr., 'Bernal's "Blacks" and the Afrocentrists', in *Black Athena Revisited*, ed. Mary Lefkowitz and Guy MacLean Rogers (Chapel Hill and London: University of North Carolina Press, 1996), 112–28.

Spencer, T. J. B., *Shakespeare: The Roman Plays*, Writers and Their Work 157, British Council and the National Book League (London: Longmans, Green & Co., 1963).

—— (ed.), *Shakespeare's Plutarch* (Harmondsworth: Penguin, 1964).

Spevack, Marvin, *A New Variorum Edition of Shakespeare's 'Antony and Cleopatra'* (New York: The Modern Language Association of America, 1991).

Stempel, Daniel, 'The Transmigration of the Crocodile', *SQ*, 7 (1956).

Stoll, E. E., *Poets and Playwrights* (Minneapolis: University of Minnesota Press, 1930).

Swinburne, Algernon Charles, *A Study of Shakespeare* (1880; London: Chatto & Windus, 1902).

Thomas, Vivian, *Shakespeare's Roman Worlds* (London: Routledge, 1989).

Thompson, J. A. K., *Shakespeare and the Classics* (London: Allen & Unwin, 1952).

Ulrici, Hermann, *Shakespeare's Dramatic Art* (1839; 2nd ed. 1847; 3rd edn. 1868–9), trans. from 3rd German ed. by Dora L. Schmitz, 2 vols (1876).

Volkmann, Hans, *Cleopatra: A study in Politics and Propaganda*, trans. J. Cadoux (London: Elek, 1953).

Weitz, Morris, 'Literature without Philosophy: *Antony and Cleopatra*', *Shakespeare Survey*, 28 (1975), 29–36.

Wimsatt Jr., W. K., *The Verbal Icon* (Lexington, KY: University of Kentucky Press, 1954).

Woodbridge, Linda, *Women and the English Renaissance: Literature and the Nature of Womankind, 1540–1620* (Urbana: University of Illinois Press; Brighton: Harvester, 1984).

Index

Recent and Forthcoming Titles in the New Series of

WRITERS AND THEIR WORK

WRITERS AND THEIR WORK

RECENT & FORTHCOMING TITLES

Title	Author
Chinua Achebe	*Nahem Yousaf*
Peter Ackroyd	*Susana Onega*
Kingsley Amis	*Richard Bradford*
Anglo-Saxon Verse	*Graham Holderness*
Antony and Cleopatra 2/e	*Ken Parker*
As You Like It	*Penny Gay*
W. H. Auden	*Stan Smith*
Jane Austen	*Robert Miles*
Alan Ayckbourn	*Michael Holt*
J. G. Ballard	*Michel Delville*
Pat Barker	*Sharon Monteith*
Djuna Barnes	*Deborah Parsons*
Julian Barnes	*Matthew Pateman*
Samuel Beckett	*Sinead Mooney*
Aphra Behn 2/e	*S. J. Wiseman*
John Betjeman	*Dennis Brown*
William Blake	*Steven Vine*
Edward Bond	*Michael Mangan*
Anne Brontë	*Betty Jay*
Emily Brontë	*Stevie Davies*
Robert Browning	*John Woodford*
A. S. Byatt	*Richard Todd*
Byron	*Drummond Bone*
Caroline Drama	*Julie Sanders*
Angela Carter 2/e	*Lorna Sage*
Bruce Chatwin	*Kerry Featherstone*
Geoffrey Chaucer	*Steve Ellis*
Children's Literature	*Kimberley Reynolds*
Children's Writers of the 19th Century	*Mary Sebag-Montefiore*
Caryl Churchill 2/e	*Elaine Aston*
John Clare	*John Lucas*
S. T. Coleridge	*Stephen Bygrave*
Joseph Conrad	*Cedric Watts*
Coriolanus	*Anita Pacheco*
Stephen Crane	*Kevin Hayes*
Crime Fiction	*Martin Priestman*
Anita Desai	*Elaine Ho*
Shashi Deshpande	*Amrita Bhalla*
Charles Dickens	*Rod Mengham*
John Donne	*Stevie Davies*
Margaret Drabble	*Glenda Leeming*
John Dryden	*David Hopkins*
Carol Ann Duffy 2/e	*Deryn Rees Jones*
Early Modern Sonneteers	*Michael Spiller*
George Eliot	*Josephine McDonagh*
T. S. Eliot	*Colin MacCabe*
English Translators of Homer	*Simeon Underwood*
Henry Fielding	*Jenny Uglow*
Veronica Forrest-Thomson – Language Poetry	*Alison Mark*
E. M. Forster	*Nicholas Royle*

RECENT & FORTHCOMING TITLES

Title	Author
John Fowles	*William Stephenson*
Brian Friel	*Geraldine Higgins*
Athol Fugard	*Dennis Walder*
Elizabeth Gaskell	*Kate Flint*
The *Gawain*-Poet	*John Burrow*
The Georgian Poets	*Rennie Parker*
William Golding 2/e	*Kevin McCarron*
Graham Greene	*Peter Mudford*
Neil M. Gunn	*J. B. Pick*
Ivor Gurney	*John Lucas*
Hamlet 2/e	*Ann Thompson & Neil Taylor*
Thomas Hardy 2/e	*Peter Widdowson*
Tony Harrison	*Joe Kelleher*
William Hazlitt	*J. B. Priestley; R. L. Brett (intro. by Michael Foot)*
Seamus Heaney 2/e	*Andrew Murphy*
George Herbert	*T.S. Eliot (intro. by Peter Porter)*
Geoffrey Hill	*Andrew Roberts*
Gerard Manley Hopkins	*Daniel Brown*
Henrik Ibsen 2/e	*Sally Ledger*
Kazuo Ishiguro 2/e	*Cynthia Wong*
Henry James – The Later Writing	*Barbara Hardy*
James Joyce 2/e	*Steven Connor*
Julius Caesar	*Mary Hamer*
Franz Kafka	*Michael Wood*
John Keats	*Kelvin Everest*
James Kelman	*Gustav Klaus*
Hanif Kureishi	*Ruvani Ranasinha*
Samuel Johnson	*Liz Bellamy*
William Langland: *Piers Plowman*	*Claire Marshall*
King Lear	*Terence Hawkes*
Philip Larkin 2/e	*Laurence Lerner*
D. H. Lawrence	*Linda Ruth Williams*
Doris Lessing	*Elizabeth Maslen*
C. S. Lewis	*William Gray*
Wyndham Lewis and Modernism	*Andrzej Gasiorek*
David Lodge	*Bernard Bergonzi*
Katherine Mansfield	*Andrew Bennett*
Christopher Marlowe	*Thomas Healy*
Andrew Marvell	*Annabel Patterson*
Ian McEwan 2/e	*Kiernan Ryan*
Measure for Measure	*Kate Chedgzoy*
The Merchant of Venice	*Warren Chernaik*
A Midsummer Night's Dream	*Helen Hackett*
Alice Munro	*Ailsa Cox*
Vladimir Nabokov	*Neil Cornwell*
V. S. Naipaul	*Suman Gupta*
Grace Nichols	*Sarah Lawson-Welsh*
Edna O'Brien	*Amanda Greenwood*
Flann O'Brien	*Joe Brooker*
Ben Okri	*Robert Fraser*
George Orwell	*Douglas Kerr*
Othello	*Emma Smith*
Walter Pater	*Laurel Brake*

Title	Author
Brian Patten	*Linda Cookson*
Caryl Phillips	*Helen Thomas*
Harold Pinter	*Mark Batty*
Sylvia Plath 2/e	*Elisabeth Bronfen*
Pope Amongst the Satirists	*Brean Hammond*
Revenge Tragedies of the Renaissance	*Janet Clare*
Jean Rhys 2/e	*Helen Carr*
Richard II	*Margaret Healy*
Richard III	*Edward Burns*
Dorothy Richardson	*Carol Watts*
John Wilmot, Earl of Rochester	*Germaine Greer*
Romeo and Juliet	*Sasha Roberts*
Christina Rossetti	*Kathryn Burlinson*
Salman Rushdie 2/e	*Damian Grant*
Paul Scott	*Jacqueline Banerjee*
The Sensation Novel	*Lyn Pykett*
P. B. Shelley	*Paul Hamilton*
Sir Walter Scott	*Harriet Harvey Wood*
Iain Sinclair	*Robert Sheppard*
Christopher Smart	*Neil Curry*
Wole Soyinka	*Mpalive Msiska*
Muriel Spark	*Brian Cheyette*
Edmund Spenser	*Colin Burrow*
Gertrude Stein	*Nicola Shaughnessy*
Laurence Sterne	*Manfred Pfister*
Bram Stoker	*Andrew Maunder*
Graham Swift	*Peter Widdowson*
Jonathan Swift	*Ian Higgins*
Swinburne	*Catherine Maxwell*
Alfred Tennyson	*Seamus Perry*
W. M. Thackeray	*Richard Salmon*
D. M. Thomas	*Bran Nicol*
J. R. R. Tolkien	*Charles Moseley*
Leo Tolstoy	*John Bayley*
Charles Tomlinson	*Tim Clark*
Anthony Trollope	*Andrew Sanders*
Victorian Quest Romance	*Robert Fraser*
Marina Warner	*Laurence Coupe*
Edith Wharton	*Janet Beer*
Oscar Wilde	*Alexandra Warrick*
Angus Wilson	*Peter Conradi*
Mary Wollstonecraft	*Jane Moore*
Women's Gothic 2/e	*E. J. Clery*
Women Poets of the 19th Century	*Emma Mason*
Women Romantic Poets	*Anne Janowitz*
Women Writers of the 17th Century	*Ramona Wray*
Virginia Woolf 2/e	*Laura Marcus*
Working Class Fiction	*Ian Haywood*
W. B. Yeats	*Edward Larrissy*
Charlotte Yonge	*Alethea Hayter*

TITLES IN PREPARATION

Title   Author

Fleur Adcock	*Janet Wilson*
Ama Ata Aidoo	*Nana Wilson-Tagoe*
Matthew Arnold	*Kate Campbell*
Margaret Atwood	*Marion Wynne-Davies*
John Banville	*Peter Dempsey*
William Barnes	*Christopher Ricks*
Black British Writers	*Deidre Osborne*
Charlotte Brontë	*Stevie Davies*
Basil Bunting	*Martin Stannard*
John Bunyan	*Tamsin Spargoe*
Cymbeline	*Peter Swaab*
Douglas Dunn	*David Kennedy*
David Edgar	*Peter Boxall*
J. G. Farrell	*John McLeod*
Nadine Gordimer	*Lewis Nkosi*
Geoffrey Grigson	*R. M. Healey*
David Hare	*Jeremy Ridgman*
Ted Hughes	*Susan Bassnett*
The Imagist Poets	*Andrew Thacker*
Ben Jonson	*Anthony Johnson*
A. L. Kennedy	*Dorothy McMillan*
Jack Kerouac	*Michael Hrebebiak*
Jamaica Kincaid	*Susheila Nasta*
Rudyard Kipling	*Jan Montefiore*
Rosamond Lehmann	*Judy Simon*
Una Marson & Louise Bennett	*Alison Donnell*
Norman MacCaig	*Alasdair Macrae*
Thomas Middleton	*Hutchings & Bromham*
John Milton	*Nigel Smith*
Much Ado About Nothing	*John Wilders*
R. K. Narayan	*Shirley Chew*
New Woman Writers	*Marion Shaw/Lyssa Randolph*
Ngugi wa Thiong'o	*Brendon Nicholls*
Religious Poets of the 17th Century	*Helen Wilcox*
Samuel Richardson	*David Deeming*
Olive Schreiner	*Carolyn Burdett*
Sam Selvon	*Ramchand & Salick*
Olive Senior	*Denise de Canes Narain*
Mary Shelley	*Catherine Sharrock*
Charlotte Smith & Helen Williams	*Angela Keane*
R. L. Stevenson	*David Robb*
Tom Stoppard	*Nicholas Cadden*
Elizabeth Taylor	*N. R. Reeve*
Dylan Thomas	*Chris Wiggington*
Three Avant-Garde Poets	*Peter Middleton*
Three Lyric Poets	*William Rowe*
Derek Walcott	*Stephen Regan*
Jeanette Winterson	*Gina Vitello*
Women's Poetry at the Fin de Siècle	*Anna Vadillo*
William Wordsworth	*Nicola Trott*